Shift Your Career into High Gear

LOIS MORAN

Cover Design by JuLee Brand / designchik

Author photos by Niño Gallego Studios

Career VOLTA / Lois Moran —1st ed.

Paperback ISBN 978-1-7325598-0-6

eBook ISBN 978-1-7325598-1-3

DEDICATION

A legacy of moxie. My grandmother, mother, and great-grandmother–each one an accomplished, industrious woman in her own right.

THIS BOOK IS DEDICATED TO 3 POWERFUL WOMEN. They aren't famous, they're not celebrities, but for me they are larger than life.

MARY IS MY GREAT-GRANDMOTHER. In the late 1800s she boarded a boat in Sicily and alongside her mother and brother made her way across the Atlantic. After gaining passage through Ellis Island, they settled in the Little Italy section of NYC. Mary insisted that women needed a trade—something that generated a reliable income. During the Great Depression, her job at the coat factory was secure because she was one of their best hand-sewing finishers. During those lean years, she was the only one in her family with a paycheck. This covered the rent and provided "plenty of soup and bread on the table."

CONNIE IS MY GRANDMOTHER. She lived on 9th Avenue in NYC, "over where they were building the Lincoln Tunnel." On the insistence of her mother, she became a dressmaker. Her pay was calculated "by the dress." The ceiling literally vibrated from the horsepower of her home-based "backup" sewing machine. I cherished every moment I spent with her. She loved to work. She loved people, books, and accessories—and she loved tracking her investments in the stock market!

JOSEPHINE IS MY MOTHER. She was born in Brooklyn, NY. From there she moved to NYC—she and her family eventually moved across the Hudson River "to the country," Staten Island. At a mere 5'2" she was the captain of her all-girl Catholic high school's basketball team. (What does that tell you?) All I know is that she gave those nuns a run for their money! She too is a wizard at the sewing machine, but she opted for the college route instead, ultimately earning her MBA.

I am blessed by the lineage of these three larger-than-life women. I feel them in my spirit. I hold them in my heart. Strong. Vibrant. Fearless. Unstoppable. They are my inspiration.

ABOUT THE AUTHOR

LOIS MORAN is a career woman, entrepreneur, and success-maker. She draws from a unique base of experience that began over 20 years ago in corporate America. It all started with two Fortune 500 pharmaceutical companies: GSK (formerly SK&F), followed by Merck (formerly Schering-Plough). Lois then crossed over to agency life, which culminated in the co-founding of JUICE Pharma Worldwide, where she served as CEO of the New York City office for 15 years. Lois is impassioned to help women get into the driver's seat of their careers. Her confidence-building programs are designed to spark illuminations and action plans that bring life-transforming VOLTAs. Lois's courage and resolve are rooted in her faith and her family.

CONTENTS

INTRODUCTION

I will never forget my first career VOLTA.

It started on a Friday. I had *finally* landed one of the coveted positions on the Marketing Team. It was my first presentation to the top brass. This was big league. I stood there alone at the head of the mahogany conference table. My PowerPoint deck was loaded and on screen. Almost every seat on each side of the table was occupied. As I looked down the table, which seemed to go on forever, all eyes were on me. All men. Smart, accomplished, marketers. Every one of them. I can remember that my vision was a little blurry. My heart was pounding. I could hear my pulse swishing in my ears.

My new boss was there too. The "robot." I noticed that he didn't select the seat that was closest to where I was standing. He hadn't offered to help me prepare for this either. *No problem.* I was ready.

But I bombed. Their questions kept coming, one after the other. *What were your market share and sales at this time last year? What's happening with the launch of Glaxo's new nasal steroid? What is your current sample inventory? What are you forecasting for the upcoming fall season? What have you heard from the sales force about the coupon program? What is your projected sales evolution index?*

I tried to keep it together. Truth is, I didn't know the answer to many of their questions. (For crying out loud, this was my first position in Marketing–I had been there less than a month.) When the torture ended I took my seat at the table. Their cold disapproval was palpable, hanging heavy in the air. Waves of humiliation washed over me. I could barely breathe.

I had to get out of there. But, as it turned out, the torture wasn't over yet. It continued as I sat at the table, listening to each of the smooth-talking marketing menfolk present their very polished business updates. They presented with confidence and with ease. Their presentations were also perfectly peppered with well-placed humor.

That weekend, my mind replayed the scene over and over again. Shame cut its way deep into to my core.

By Sunday night, something that I learned from my mother *finally* kicked in. Josephine is a force to be reckoned with. She taught me by example–to take responsibility for my failings, to get up, and to keep going. So after this very long weekend, marked by tears of shame and anger, I made myself push forward into resolve-mode. I had to become the person my mother raised me to be, again.

It was a moment of truth. I pressed the pause button to reflect upon my situation. *What was I going to do to reckon with this situation? How was I going to go back and face everyone?* I made a decision. I would work my butt off to become 110% immersed in my business. I would know everything about my brands–sales and market share trends, forecasting and inventory, sales rep feedback, market research insights, and the competitive landscape. I would become the expert. I would become the "one to watch."

I vowed to myself: *This will never happen to me again, so help me God.* It was at that moment that I got into the driver's seat of my career, took a firm hold of the steering wheel, and drove with purpose and with confidence toward my new destiny. Did I mention that I was six months pregnant?

Fast forward 20 years

I made the decision to write this book–another VOLTA moment.

I was at a hotel in Barcelona on the rooftop terrace after a productive day collaborating with a very accomplished digital agency. Maybe it was how the light in Spain seeped into my soul. Maybe it was where I was in my life journey. Or perhaps it was because my daughter, Meredith, was about to graduate college and enter the workforce. I can't say for sure. One thing was certain–something unstoppable had been stirred up deep within me.

It was the beginning of my obsession to share my struggles as a career woman with other career women so that I could be of service to them. Like a dog on a bone, I set out on a course to catalogue *every* meaningful lesson that I'd had to learn over the past three decades. I wasn't someone who was "born with it." Who really is? I had to *learn* everything. I had to learn how to be taken seriously, I had to learn how to be heard, and I had to learn how to have unmistakable presence.

I wrote this book because I want you to have a resource that I didn't have.

I want you to slide into the driver's seat of your career and grab hold of *everything* you aspire to be. With *Career VOLTA*, you will have the competitive edge that you need to succeed–all in one place.

Perhaps this book caught your eye because *you want more* out of your career: more success, more responsibility, more joy.

If that's the case–and you can relate to one or more of the scenarios below–consider buying and reading this book as a gift to yourself:

- You feel stuck in your career
- You want to be more confident and to sharpen your skills
- You want to be more promotable
- You want to re-enter the work force
- You want to make a career change
- You're a leader who wants to help her team excel

Why take my advice when it comes to *your* career?

I'm not a therapist. I do not have a PhD. But I do have extensive firsthand experience that comes from spending many years in corporate America, and from owning and running a multimillion-dollar advertising company.

I'm also a curator–I read and consume a lot of information, every day. (And so should you.) In addition to sharing my experience and wisdom, I have added what I believe to be inspiring insights from many other top-notch resources. This is a *reading adventure* that you will emerge from feeling revitalized and empowered.

I can be a behind-the-curtain, trusted resource for you because:

- I *learned* my way to the top.
- I've had many opportunities to figure out what works—and what doesn't.
- I bring a rich tapestry of stories–stories of failure, struggles, and victories.
- I want career women to have everything they need to succeed with confidence, and with joy, in the business world.

And because of what I have achieved...

For 15 years, I was a co-owner and CEO of JUICE Pharma Worldwide, a multimillion-dollar healthcare advertising agency headquartered in New York City, with billings that grew to over $50 million for five years in a row. At our peak, we had over 200 employees. Together we won numerous awards and numerous pitches against some very impressive competitors such as the mighty Omnicom. We had the honor of building well-known megabrands such as Singulair and Gardasil. For these and other achievements, JUICE was nominated "Agency of the Year" two years in a row.

Before co-founding JUICE, I had crossed over to the agency side for several years. Advertising agency life is fascinating. It's one of those rare environments that lets you combine your technical knowledge with your love for business through the implementation of behavior-changing words and visuals. Advertising agencies are a place where your demographic doesn't really matter. If you're talented and you work hard, your career can skyrocket. I went from VP of Account to SVP Account in less than two years. It was during my tenure with Foot Cone & Belding (FCB) where I learned the fine art of client services—tripling my fees from $3M to almost $9M. And it was at FCB where I met my extraordinary business partners.

For the first 10 years of my career, I clawed my way up the corporate ladder at two different Fortune 500 pharmaceutical companies–first with GSK (formerly SK&F) and then with Merck (formerly Schering-Plough). I started out as a junior medical writer and very purposefully navigated my way to become a team leader by the age of 25. When I figured out that decision-making and budget power resided with Marketing and not with Medical, I set my sights on getting into Marketing. I soon found out that this wasn't going to be as easy as I had hoped.

In order to advance one step closer to a position in Marketing, I petitioned hard for an opening as a state lobbyist. In this position, I was responsible for affecting policy and legislation related to the pharmaceutical industry in 11 states. As a state lobbyist I became a road warrior. I learned the ins and the outs of weekly business trips, I learned how to live out of a suitcase and still look crisp, and I learned how to "schmooze." I worked the room, I mingled, hobnobbed, and networked. At 26, my schmoozing skills were awful. But, as with many things, I got better at it with practice and, as you can imagine, this skill came in handy many times down the road.

Being a state lobbyist wasn't a position that I relished, but it paid off because it became the stepping stone to my first marketing position.

The day I arrived in Marketing I was greeted by the all-boys club. The Sharks. Let's just say that I had a lot to learn. I found out pretty quickly that I was very naïve and that these Sharks were shrewd. They were fierce competitors with highly functioning support systems. At work, they had their "advocates" and at home, they had someone to make their meals and to run their suits to the dry cleaner.

I had finally *arrived* but it was like getting hit with cold water in the face. It was a rude awakening. It was a proving ground. And it was one of the most influential times in my career.

I have to admit that I learned a lot from The Sharks. They were impressive. They seemed to operate on instinct. I wanted what they had. I watched them in action, and when I was ready, I went into direct hand-to-hand combat with them. We debated during lunch. We outmaneuvered one another as we vied for marketing dollars. We competed fiercely for the sales forces' attention with clever bonus programs. During that time I became close friends with several of them—and I earned respect from all of them. On this long and clunky road–of many highs and lows–I *learned* my way to becoming one of the few female director-level leaders with the Schering-Plough Marketing Team. There I led and launched several brands related to dermatology, allergy, and then asthma. I managed multimillion-dollar advertising, PR, and media budgets. I was responsible for sales growth and for manufacturing forecasting. I was also responsible for motivating and garnering the love and attention for my brands from a sales force of over 5,000. In addition, I was charged with finding new licensing opportunities and for establishing trust-based relationships with thought leaders in the industry.

During those formative years, I evolved into a full-fledged career woman. It was exhilarating, and at times, exhausting. But I was determined. Determined to overcome, to make my mark, to be successful.

Are you ready for *your* career VOLTA?

VOLTA originated from Shakespearean sonnets. VOLTAs are sudden recognitions that transform our understanding of what we are truly capable of. When you have a VOLTA it's a defining moment in your life. Think of it as a process. First, you press pause–or to continue with the driving analogy, you hit the brakes–to reflect upon your current situation. You will be illuminated by something significant about yourself or your situation. This illumination will trigger your resolve to *shift* into action.

PAUSE + ILLUMINATION + TAKE ACTION = VOLTA

This is a time in your life that you will always remember. The roadblocks that may be holding you back, such as fear, confusion, or a lack of confidence–are replaced with a fierce determination. **This is when you will deliberately get into the driver's seat of your life–in this case, your career life.**

Your inner dialogue will now become a source of forward momentum by saying things like *I'm not going to feel like this anymore! I can do this! I'm worth it!*

The science behind a VOLTA

When you're having a VOLTA, the right hemisphere of your brain literally lights up with what John Kounios, author of *The Eureka Factor*, refers to as the "insight effect." This insight effect moves you to reckon with the things that are blocking your path. You will feel stronger than ever because what's happening to you is actually neurological.

You will shift:
From confusion to clarity.
From hesitation to confidence.
From stuck to driving forward.

We will go on an illuminating 3-step journey together

My commitment to you is to take you by the hand and guide you through the *Career VOLTA* process. I will serve as your tough-but-loving coach equipping you to move forward with bold confidence to attain your career aspirations.

Career VOLTA offers a unique 3-step process that comes with all of the tools you will need to drive you forward in your career.

In Part 1, the first step, you will press pause and take stock of where you are, right now, with the 5 VOLTA Awakenings. These 5 Awakenings will illuminate self-discovery through reflective exercises designed to spark actionable epiphanies. This will help you to release any baggage–limiting beliefs–you might be carrying around with you.

In Part 2, the second step, you will see for yourself where you are on the spectrum of the *must-haves* for career success. These are the 5 VOLTA Trade Secrets. Complete with these secrets and how-tos, you will become fully equipped with the most important methods and techniques to fuel your career momentum. Each of the 5 Trade Secrets comes with a self-assessment tool that will let you measure your progress as you weave these best practices into your career life.

In Part 3, the final step, you will be ready to pull together everything you have learned about yourself–and your heart's desires–into the building of your own VOLTA Career Plan. Here you will align your renewed vision for yourself with a plan of action for making your new vision a *reality.*

Put *Career VOLTA* to work for you. Let this book be a catalyst and a touchstone that you can return to each and every time you need it. Let me guide you on this transformative journey. Your confidence will soar–and the career that you want for yourself will be yours. As my mother often declares (I'm pretty sure she borrowed this from Shakespeare):

> "The world is your oyster!"

BEFORE YOU BEGIN

PRESSING PAUSE

WHAT'S YOUR *WHY?*

WHAT'S YOUR *WHY*?

Before you start and commit to your *Career VOLTA* journey—you need to know your *why.*

Tony Robbins refers to our *why* as the emotional juice that keeps us going—the force that pulls us forward—a force that doesn't depend on willpower. Willpower is a force that pushes us. Our *why* is the ***pull.*** It's what we're willing to fight for, work for, and grind for.

When it comes to this pulling force, motivational speaker Eric Thomas literally gets right up in your face with this challenge:

> " Life is going to hit you in your mouth.
> Is your *why* greater than that punch? "

Figuring out your *why* is a concept that many of us—life coaches, motivational speakers, and self-help gurus–give a lot of attention to. Books like *Start With Why* by Simon Sinek and Kent Burns' *What's Your Why* explore how we are wired to go after the life-changing fulfillment that comes from following our unique passion and purpose.

So what is your *why*—the unstoppable force that's driving your career VOLTA?

My *why* was fueled by a deep, visceral need to prove my worthiness. I was hell-bent on proving that I was just as qualified as my male counterparts to be responsible for multimillion-dollar pharmaceutical brands. I was determined to become a worthy contender. To be taken seriously. Not to be ignored. Not to be invisible.

My *why* hasn't changed. It's still the same:

> **I want career women to be highly visible contenders to be taken seriously and respected—because they've earned it.**

As you consider your *why*—your pulling force—reflect on these possibilities:

- Is there something that you have to prove to yourself?
- Is there something that you have to prove to someone else?
- Is there someone in your life who you want to honor?
- Is there someone counting on you to succeed?
- Are you fighting for financial security or independence?
- Are you showing your parents that their investment in you was worth it?
- Are you yearning for creative expression or creative release?
- Are you striving for something greater than yourself?

It's time to **declare your *why*.** Write it down in the space provided—and let it be the "emotional juice" that fuels your journey.

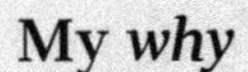

My *why*

The unstoppable force that's driving me forward is...

How does figuring out your *why* help you? It's actually very simple: **You will need it.** Your *why* is why you struggle. Your why is why you get up every time you fall. Your *why* is why you will continue to press on—even when things seem impossible. There will be times when you have to remind yourself of your *why*, as you are fighting for your career dreams.

Always know your *why*. Keep it front and center.

PART 1

YOUR 5 VOLTA AWAKENINGS

WHAT GOT YOU HERE?

“Knowing yourself is the beginning of all wisdom.”

ARISTOTLE

THERE ARE DYNAMICS IN THE WORKPLACE that are out of your control—and yes, they can present real challenges to your ability, as a woman, to attain career success. For example, working in an environment where you are an exception to the rule—such as being a woman among a sea of men. This can be vexing. However, in order for you to be in the driver's seat of your career, it's very important to acknowledge and to believe that *you* play the *most central role* in your career advancement.

I find this outlook to be both comforting and invigorating because it places the power to affect our career destinies *directly* into our own hands.

Career VOLTA will help you find self-awareness and confidence that will stand the test of time. It will help you to become your own best friend—which is fertile ground for enormous career power.

The primary objective of Part 1 is for you to go on a self-discovery road trip. This is the first phase of the *Career VOLTA* process. In the words of Brendon Burchard, the bestselling author of *High Performance Habits*:

> "I've found that the first step is always [self] awareness."

My personal VOLTA self-discovery journey taught me this: When I peel back the layers of self-protection to get to the truth, I find that it's not what people are doing to me, but rather, it's *what I am doing to myself* that really matters.

THE 5 VOLTA AWAKENINGS WILL HELP YOU TAKE STOCK OF YOUR INNER SELF AND YOUR OUTER SELF

The 5 VOLTA Awakenings have been choice-fully selected and organized to start your *Career VOLTA* journey on the right foot. I believe these 5 Awakenings have the greatest potential to impact your career life.

The empowerment that comes with "knowing thyself" will accelerate your career advancement and your personal satisfaction.

To bring simplicity to this self-discovery phase, I employed a well-recognized model that includes two domains of the self, the *inner self* and the *outer self.* In this model, the inner self includes the unseen things that live in your head, such as: how you think, what you believe, and what you tell yourself. Cleo Wade, poet, artist, speaker, says it best:

> “It's a lot easier to take care of your outer self if your inner self is taken care of.”

The outer self refers to what you project—how people see you and how they experience you—based on your behavior, how you present yourself, and your packaging.

Take heart; most of our beliefs and behaviors become established before we even reach the age of two. Oftentimes, simply *gaining awareness* of these ingrained beliefs and behaviors is all we need to have a breakthrough.

To experience these breakthroughs, I will help you take stock of your inner self on several significant fronts starting with an understanding of your current mindset—where I will reveal a big choice that you must make for yourself. We will then have you take a listen to your inner dialogue to see if it needs a tune-up. Next we will delve in and unpack any fears and stressors that could be getting in the way of the career you want. Then we will move forward to identify any energy-drainers that you need to address or remove from your path.

Once you have gained actionable awareness of any inner roadblocks, I will help you take stock of your outer self—what you are projecting and how others are seeing and experiencing you. We will work to give you a very clear and actionable picture of your outward-facing self by taking inventory of your brand so that you're able to make any necessary adjustments.

Are you ready to roll up your sleeves and dig in?

VOLTA AWAKENING

#1

SHIFTING INTO THE SUCCESS MINDSET

Is your current mindset helping you, or is it limiting your career success?

I became fast friends with a gal who was one of the few female members on the marketing team with me. I loved her vitality and her bodacious attitude. She drove a bright red Volvo. Many times in the morning we would spot each other driving north on the Garden State Parkway on the way to work. She would pull up alongside me and flash her hallmark smile. Then she'd hit the gas and speed off to Exit 138 Kenilworth.

Her car was a gift that she gave to herself. In fact, every time she got a promotion, she bought herself a *very* significant gift. Truth is, she was getting promotions at a noticeably faster pace than me. Maybe this had something to do with it...

I was struck and impressed by how my friend *willingly* shared her work-in-progress ideas—ad campaign concepts, draft presentation decks, and draft marketing plans. She would share these drafts with numerous people from the Marketing and Sales Teams in order to "get a read." She wanted their recommendations and their input. She was genuinely open and interested in their perspective—even when it clashed with her own. She was a bona fide, curious learner.

I wish I could have said the same for myself back then. At that time in my career I was very protective of my ideas. Any opposing opinion–especially from someone more senior than me—I internalized negatively as a setback, a criticism. I did *not* view it as something positive the way my friend did. I needed to be right, and I *certainly* never wanted to be wrong. When I finally realized the downside of this behavior, I worked hard to deliberately renounce and abandon my protective, defensive mindset.

I learned, the hard way, that if you truly want to excel as a businessperson–you must become a *curious learner.* Your ideas should be vetted, with genuine curiosity, if you want to improve them. Plus, there's an added benefit that you'll gain when you seek input *before* "the big unveiling": People readily buy into ideas that *they have already put their stamp on.* A big unveiling without obtaining this unofficial feedback along the way is risky business–and it usually doesn't go well.

I felt a little better when I read in American billionaire investor Ray Dalio's book *Principles* that, like me, he went through a similar conversion process in order to say goodbye to his *I have to be right* mindset.

Ray shared this, "Knowing that I could be painfully wrong and have curiosity about why other smart people saw things differently prompted me to look at things through the eyes of others as well as my own."

It's nice to know that I'm in good company with a billionaire.

My intention behind telling this story is to *compel you* to ask yourself this very important question:

Is your current mindset helping you, or is it limiting your career success?

Research has landed rather firmly on the fact that there are only **two mindsets.** And you need to know where *you* currently stand with respect to these two mindsets, because it is one of the most crucial factors that drives career success and happiness in life. If you want to experience something that can be life-changing, you're going to have to be *really honest* with yourself as you're reading this chapter.

Mindset is defined as a person's prevailing mental state, their attitude or disposition that predetermines their responses to and their interpretations of situations. Your mindset drives your behavior and your actions. Our mindset can make a *big* difference in how we experience life. The wrong mindset can drag you down, like a heavy weight around your ankles. The right mindset is freeing, a state of existence that's uplifting and sparkling with optimism.

There is an abundance of provocative information on the topic of mindset. My research has revealed a common theme among the thought leaders in the field. In their own ways, with their own methods of discovery, they have *all* drawn the same conclusion—that there are only two mindset categories.

For example, in her pioneering book, *Mindset*, Carol Dweck outlines that you fall within either the "fixed" or the "growth" mindset. That's it, she asserts: no in-betweens. Dr. Joe Dispenza takes up the concept of mindset in *Breaking the Habit of Being Yourself*, and he too believes that people fall into one of two categories—he coined the terms "survival" and "creation" mindsets. In *The Telomere Effort*, Nobel Prize-winning molecular biologist Elizabeth Blackburn and health psychologist Elissa Epel describe the two mindsets as "negative threat-based" and "positive challenge-based."

For me, I like to think of these two mindset camps as Camp A: I'm Hard On Myself and Camp B: I'm A Work In Progress.

The characteristics of Camp A: I'm Hard On Myself describe a mental state where we find ourselves feeling like we need to have all the answers; we are uncomfortable making mistakes; we find it difficult to move swiftly forward after a failure. Camp A members strive for perfection. At times, they can come across as defensive. According to Dweck, this happens because they are protecting their identity, without even realizing it.

Those in Camp B: I'm A Work In Progress hold the belief that failure is often the best catalyst for accomplishment. People with this mindset believe that it's okay to be continuously learning and evolving. They tend to be able to shake off mistakes and setbacks quickly and move forward with purposeful optimism. This is what allows them to live in a mental state of "Bring it on!" They embrace the humanness of themselves and others—they are able to enjoy themselves and others more. As a way to remind yourself that Camp B is *the* place to live, think of the "B" as standing for something like "Better" or "Bring it on" or even as Jen Sincero would say "Badass."

Here comes the hard truth. Based on my firsthand experience over many years of coaching lots of women, I have found that many women tend to reside in Camp A—especially when facing stressful situations. The problem is that it's hard to admit that we reside in Camp A, and if we can't see or admit that about ourselves, how can we hope to move beyond this mindset? The Camp B mindset is a far better place to live. It is characterized by *self-compassion* and a greater receptivity to learning from our mistakes and moving forward from life's setbacks. And it opens the door to having more fun!

So, let's take a few moments to consider what this comparison looks like.

THE TWO MINDSET CAMPS

	CAMP A: I'M HARD ON MYSELF	**CAMP B: I'M A WORK IN PROGRESS**
How others might describe you	Intense Serious Driven	Curious Humble Driven
Your belief about your intellect	My intelligence is a fixed quality	My intelligence can be developed
Your belief about your abilities	I've reached my full potential	My true potential is unknown
Your inner dialogue	I must get this right	I'll figure it out
How you feel when challenged	Uncomfortable	Excited
How you treat yourself	A bit tough on yourself	Able to laugh at yourself

Be really honest with yourself: Which camp do you live in most of the time? It is important to answer this question in the framework of when your mindset matters the most—that is, the times *when you are faced with a new or stressful situation.* I'm not referring to when you are chugging along with routine matters.

EXERCISE #1:

WHAT MINDSET CAMP DO YOU LIVE IN?

- Imagine yourself in a recent challenging work-related situation. This could be a new experience that you've recently faced, or a recurring trigger event that continues to cause you stress.
- With the chart below, hold this memory close as you check the appropriate boxes that most honestly reflect how you felt or reacted.

THE TWO MINDSET CAMPS

	CAMP A: I'M HARD ON MYSELF	✓	CAMP B: I'M A WORK IN PROGRESS	✓
How others might describe you	Intense Serious Driven		Curious Humble Driven	
Your belief about your intellect	My intelligence is a fixed quality		My intelligence can be developed	
Your belief about your abilities	I've reached my full potential		My true potential is unknown	
Your inner dialogue	I must get this right		I'll figure it out	
How you feel when challenged	Uncomfortable		Excited	
How you treat yourself	A bit tough on yourself		Able to laugh at yourself	

YOU CAN CHANGE YOUR MINDSET

Here's the good news, ladies: If you find that you're tending more toward Camp A (like I was for many years), it's going to be okay. You're in good company, and there are things you can do to press into the more self-compassionate Camp B. Here's the thing. I find this whole topic of two mindset camps to be rather deep and complex. I mean, seriously, who the heck would actively and purposely choose to live in Camp A?! I didn't realize I was having such harsh thoughts about myself–thoughts that Carol Dweck describes as coming with a fixed mindset. Thoughts like: "My qualities are carved in stone," and that I have "an urgency to prove myself over and over," and that every situation I encounter is "an evaluation of: *Will I succeed?* or *Will I fail?*" But that's exactly where I camped out for many years.

Of course I would rather live in the *other* camp—the growth mindset camp—where one believes that "their true potential is unknown" and where "the hand you're dealt is just the starting point for development" and it's the place "where everyone can change and grow through application and experience." What a positive, uplifting belief system to live by. Who wouldn't want more of that?

Actually it's something that we can all have. In her book, Carol Dweck helps us move out of our fixed mindset into a growth mindset with numerous insightful methods and practices. Take a look at some of my favorites:

- Think about all you have learned from each of your setbacks and failures
- Think in terms of your accomplishments (this is a growth perspective) vs. your abilities (this is a fixed perspective)
- Purposely seek out constructive criticism

I strongly recommend that you read her book, *Mindset: The New Psychology of Success.* It's a life-changer.

Note: Food for thought...take these insights that you now have regarding Camp A and Camp B and think about the people around you. What camp do they live in? What camp does your boss live in? When you're interviewing for a job, what camp do you think the hiring manager falls into? How about the person sitting in front of you whom you're thinking about hiring?

My quest for myself–and for all women–is to give ourselves permission to make mistakes, to have self-compassion, and to vigorously *reject* perfectionism.

"This quest for perfection," according to Lori Bailey, global head of special lines at Zurich Insurance, "is arguably one of the biggest hurdles that many women face as they progress in their careers. It can lead to an avoidance of risk and a lack of confidence, which can put women squarely in the crossroads of advancement and opportunity." How can *you* face down your perfectionism and gain confidence? You need to *get curious.*

Turns out there is a *direct* relationship between curiosity and confidence. As we close out on mind-set and the benefits of living in curious Camp B, consider these words of wisdom...

> “Curiosity promotes creativity, creativity births confidence and confidence gives us the freedom to be our true selves.”
>
> **TRISHA BLACKWELL**

> “We can use [curiosity] to refine who we are, to help us realize that we can be more than we thought we were.”
>
> **JOANNA GAINES**

VOLTA AWAKENING

#2

REPROGRAMMING YOUR INNER DIALOGUE

You *become* what you tell yourself, so what are you telling yourself?

When I was in my mid-thirties, my marriage became unsettled. Marc was suffering from severe bouts of vertigo and I was doing a lot of overnight business travel. At the time Meredith was only four years old. The thirties can be a very stressful time in life as so many of us find ourselves juggling that delicate balance between our careers and parenting our little ones.

We weren't having heated battles–it was the opposite–our marriage had turned cold. I'm told that that the odds of recovering from a marriage gone cold are low, so we were very lucky. We were "going through the motions" living a parallel existence. We were both working very hard at our jobs, and we were both trying to be really good parents. Meredith was and will always be the apple of our eye. No matter what was going on in our lives, we've always been a united force on this front.

Marc made a decision that he was going to start going back to church. I'm pretty sure that his crippling bouts of vertigo were the trigger for his decision. He asked me if it was okay if he took Meredith with him. I was fine with that, but I chose not to join.

After several months of going to church on Sundays, Meredith started to sing hymns while she was in the bathtub. And she wouldn't just sing the songs quietly; she belted them out. Her singing bellowed up and down the halls of our Cape Cod. I wasn't sure how to react to this new phenomenon. But she was certainly happy as a little clam–and it was hard not to smile as I listened to her impassioned singing.

Within a year, I joined them. Sunday services were kicked off with 30 minutes of songs played by a seven-piece band. As I learned the words and the melodies of these songs they began to play over and over in my head–as good music has the power to do. With this came a revelation, that something had actually *stopped* playing in my head. The music had replaced the *You're not smart enough. You'll never be successful.* I wasn't aware of this inner dialogue until it *stopped* playing.

This newfound awareness was transformative for me. Not only did I learn that I *have* an inner dialogue–but I also learned that the *narrative* of my inner dialogue makes all the difference–and that it's *reprogrammable.*

What we *tell ourselves about ourselves* plays a major role in our lives, including our careers. Our inner dialogue can bring us down or it can become a source of confidence; therefore, you need to know the answer to this question for yourself:

You become what you tell yourself, so what are you telling yourself?

We all have a continuous inner dialogue—self-talk—that starts first thing in the morning and it doesn't end until we fall asleep. This is 100% normal. It's how our mind works to do things like process information and make decisions. It's also the story that we tell ourselves about ourselves day after day—as such, our inner voice is integral to our sense of self. Since we have about 65,000 thoughts per day (that's over 45 thoughts per minute if you are awake for 18 hours), it's a big advantage to have an inner dialogue that is a source of support rather than an unrelenting critic. When our inner dialogue is riddled with a steady stream of criticism and self-doubt, such as *I'm not smart enough, I don't belong here, I can't do this,* our confidence pays the price.

It's the war of voices. The battle of our inner critic vs. our inner ally. It's a matter of which one of these voices we let dominate our internal dialogue. The inner critic often brings unwelcome negative thoughts that we can keep in check with our voluntary thoughts. We need to pay close attention and press the *reprogramming* button as needed with our voluntary thoughts, because our inner critic will trigger self-doubt. We become the sum of our voluntary thoughts, so it's important that we *stop listening* to ourselves and *start talking* to ourselves.

Many highly successful women whom I know personally—and those whose memoirs I've read—have struggled with self-doubt, which usually goes hand-in-hand with negative self-talk.

Self-doubt is a confidence eroder. Women can be self-critical, and this can get in the way of our success in the workplace. We also tend to underestimate ourselves. A frequently cited Hewlett Packard internal report found that men will apply for a job or a promotion when they meet 60% of the qualifications, but women only apply when they meet 100% of them.

I am sharing this with you to get you fired up about the importance of reprogramming your inner dialogue! We need to deliberately put our inner dialogue *to work for us*. With self-awareness and some straightforward reprogramming methods, you can put your inner dialogue under "conscious control." I do this by saying to myself things like:

- *I've got this.*
- *I'm smart enough.*
- *I can lead this team.*
- *This is what I stand for.*
- *This really matters to me.*
- *This too shall pass.*
- *I am strong.*

Years ago, it was my mother who taught me that although there are many things in life that we can't control, we can control our thoughts, and we have the power to control how we react to situations. She would often make these simple, annoying, declarations that were, well, usually 100% accurate.

With practice, this method described in Exercise 2 will bring a healthier self-talk and more confidence. Actress Goldie Hawn agrees:

> "Liberation is an interesting word because you can be liberated from external things, and also from your internal dialogue."

EXERCISE #2:

TUNING INTO YOUR INNER DIALOGUE AND REDIRECTING IT TO YOUR ADVANTAGE

GETTING STARTED

- Check your calendar and designate a week where you can comfortably commit to auditing your inner dialogue every day of the week—Monday through Friday.
- Of course, you're not going to remember to do this all day long. That would be impossible and, well, strange. However, if you put yourself in "audit mode" and put thinking about your inner dialogue at the fore of your mind as often as possible, you're going to be in a position to collect very useful data about yourself.
- As you tune into the dialogue that you have with yourself, I'd like you to note four things:
  - What is the overall tone that you take with yourself?
  - What % of your inner dialogue is a negative critic vs. a supportive ally?
  - Are there any negative "themes" that your mind frequently repeats? For me, some of my repeats used to be, "You're not smart enough" and "You're in over your head" and "You're out of your league."
  - Which of these themes could be impacting your career goals?

WHAT YOU CAN EXPECT TO GAIN FROM THIS EXERCISE:

- First and foremost, you will gain awareness of your inner critic and repeating themes that you need to address.
- Second, you will now gain the ability to reprogram your inner dialogue by answering back, in a bolder inner voice:
  - *That's not who I am*
  - *That's a lie...this is the truth*
  - *I'm going to be successful on my terms*

Your inner dialogue is something that can be refocused to work for you. Since we become what we tell ourselves, imagine how unstoppable you will be when you reprogram your inner dialogue into your supportive ally. Here's a quick way to give yourself firsthand proof that your inner dialogue is a powerful resource. The next time you're at the gym, or getting ready to do something physically challenging, do what I do. Say to yourself just as you are starting: *I am strong. I can do this.* You will be amazed at how this approach will give you that extra boost of strength and confidence you need. Truth is, this simple yet highly efficacious approach can be applied to most *any* challenging situation that you are facing.

Make it a top priority to replace the negative tape that's been playing in your head with an unshakeable inner dialogue that acknowledges how far you've come. Purposely adopt an inner dialogue that inspires and motivates you to seek out your best career self.

As you are finding success in changing your inner dialogue, you can live the words of wisdom from #mondaymotivation:

> “Pay attention to your inner dialogue. That's where your life is created.”

VOLTA AWAKENING

#3

UNPACKING YOUR FEARS & STRESSORS

Are you *not* living your life because you're living your fears?

As you think about your career, if your mind is a stewpot of swirling thoughts and fears, it can boil over and cause more stress in your life. When you sprinkle in some uncertainty and anxiety, it can be, well, a nightmare.

I can only ignore these stirrings for so long until the truth bubbles up. For me, it always happens at the same time, in the same place...

It wakes me up around 3 in the morning. It's super dark and super quiet. I'm lying there in bed, usually on my side (if you sleep on your stomach, you'll get wrinkles). It never fails that my husband, Marc, is sleeping soundly, like a baby, next to me. I feel very alone. Alone with my thoughts. Alone with my inner murmurings. Alone with my fears. It's in the wee hours of the morning that the "truth" finds me—where there are no distractions to blunt the experience of being in my own head.

This happens to me a couple of times a year, so I get it. I will help you unpack these swirling thoughts and feelings so that you can examine them individually. I'm not suggesting that you will be able to eliminate all of the stressors and fears in your life. That wouldn't be realistic. But what I am saying is that when you unpack them and face each one of them, they will loosen their grip on you.

Several years ago, we encountered something that had the potential to literally cut our company in half. Talk about the need to unpack and face my fears!

Here's what happened: The procurement director from our largest client had set up a teleconference with my partners and me. We thought it was a general update because it had been snowing a lot that winter and a couple of our live meetings with her had been cancelled. We were wrong.

She dropped a bomb on us. They had made the decision to consolidate—to only work with advertising agencies that were owned by holding companies—we are independent and not owned by one of the holding companies. We stood to lose 50% of our total revenue.

As you can imagine, there were many sleepless nights. Actually, the early mornings were even worse. Waking up at 3:00am, in a cold sweat, to the blackness of February mornings. Facing some of my greatest fears: losing all of this business, having to let people go, starting all over again.

The procurement director did give us a shred of hope: If we could create a virtual network of independent agencies, led by our company, then they would consider keeping us in the mix. It was unprecedented. It had never been done in the industry. But if we could pull it off, we could save our business.

I was terrified.

Let me start by saying that I prayed a lot over these months. Every morning, I prayed alone at my dining room table for courage, for strength, and for wisdom. I also memorized this quote by Jack Canfield:

> “Your life is on the other side of what you are afraid of.”

Then one by one all of the fears and stressors were unpacked and we came up with a plan of action. The first thing my partner and I did was to meet with the procurement director to get her list of the independent agencies they were having a positive experience with. It was a list of 30-plus agencies with various areas of expertise. None of them were large-shop consumer agencies—and that was going to be a problem that had to be addressed because it would have put us at a distinct disadvantage with the competing holding companies. It was mission-critical that we mirror the offering of a holding company in order to be considered as a viable option. To do this, we knew that we had to assemble a bench of agencies for each vertical–including agencies that competed with us. There were four verticals: Scientific Promotion, Healthcare Promotion, Consumer Promotion, and Managed Care Promotion.

We knew that we had to round up all of these independent agencies and convince them to *join forces* with us to create a *virtual* holding company consisting of competing agencies. They were going to have to be willing to cooperate with us on two critical fronts—money and governance. No small task. And, per the client's direction, each of us independent agencies would have to *shed* our current identity and become part of the new collective–unified by one master agreement contract. Also, we had to reveal our sacred rate cards (pricing lists) to each other in order to create a new "universal rate card." And we all had to agree on the chain of command for this new collective—because the client wanted to make "only one phone call" for everything related to fees, annual project lists, strategic updates, and performance issues.

One by one, we called each of these agencies and presented the *opportunity.* I can remember all of the calls that I made personally like it was yesterday—where I was, what I said to coax them along, and what I said to smooth out their feathers. We were up against an impending deadline...and the human dynamics of fear, skepticism, the need to be in control, and a lack of established trust. One day, I had a pretty bad case of laryngitis so I had the husky voice of Lauren Bacall—looking back it probably helped a lot that day as I was trying to persuade the lead guy of a large consumer agency to "sign on" with us. I needed all the persuasion power I could muster.

Thankfully, many of the agencies that we reached out to were aware of this rapidly changing situation and they were predisposed to consider our proposal. They wanted to save their business, too.

Egos, control issues, and personalities had to be handled with care on the initial phone calls and during the multiple live meetings that followed. Long story short, we were able to fast track to a trusting relationship. This required a lot of intentional face time, frequent communication, and transparency. (The tray of Italian pastries that we brought to every live meeting helped too.)

We got to know about each other and each other's companies. We debated, we negotiated, and we went through many firsts together. Bottom line–we bonded. Out of need, we moved swiftly from having no relationship into a relationship of respect and trust. And, believe it or not, we made the short list. It was a miracle. This little collective of independent agencies was actually included on the short list alongside two multibillion-dollar holding companies. It was unprecedented. That year, we were invited to 13 pitches. We won back our business. All of it.

Not only that, but we forged lasting relationships with our fellow entrepreneurs that I still maintain. If I hadn't unpacked and faced down this larger-than-life fear, I wouldn't have had this enriching and rewarding life experience. It's one that I will never forget. Not ever.

So, my question for you is this:
*Are you **not** living your life because you're living your fears?*

When it comes to your fears and stressors, get in the driver's seat by unpacking them and then pressing through them, one by one.

EXERCISE #3:

UNPACKING AND SORTING OUT YOUR FEARS AND YOUR STRESSORS

I have found this exercise to be one of the most releasing, most crucial steps of the VOLTA journey. Give yourself one hour to unload everything that's been weighing on you as a tangled ball of angst. This exercise lets you release your angst in a very productive, actionable way, freeing you up to start the process of moving into a more empowered place. As you are doing this exercise, be mindful of these words from writer Robin Sharma: "The fears we don't face become our limits."

GETTING STARTED

- First, select and pre-book a day, a time, and a place that will give you one hour of complete privacy. No email, no family, no friends, nothing and nobody. This will give you the environment that's needed to completely unload. For me, it's early in the morning with a fresh cup of pressed coffee. I'm the only one awake in the house. My laptop is closed; my cell phone is out of sight.
- You will need two things: A pack of 3x5 index cards and something to write with. On each card write down one issue or item. You are going to capture everything, and I mean everything, that's causing you any stress, fear, uncertainty, hurt, anger, resentment, no matter how big or small, that is related to your career life.
- Now that you have released your baggage, you are going to rank and categorize it by sorting your cards into three categories:

CATEGORY A stressors are the things that wake you up in the middle of the night, such as not being happy in your job, getting passed over for a promotion, being unemployed, relocation, deciding whether to go back to school, and so on.

These are the things that you absolutely have to wrestle with and work through to move toward peace and joy in your career life. For example: You feel maxed out at the small company that you work for, and you really want to move from Philadelphia, but you are not sure what to pursue next.

CATEGORY B is made up of those things that are weighing on your mind, yet are less critical than your Category A's. The Category B-stressors can wait for now and often get resolved when you resolve your Category A-stressors. For example, you are struggling with a weight gain, but this could be a symptom of the disruption that your Category A-stressor is causing you.

CATEGORY C has the things that will ultimately get resolved on their own. Yes, they're adding to your current stress level, but upon closer inspection, you discover that they're only temporary. For example, you have an upcoming business trip that's going to take you away from your family over a weekend. Although this is a stressor, it will be behind you by next week. On the other hand, if your current job requires you to take frequent business trips that drag you away from your family and friends—this probably belongs in Category A.

NEXT STEPS:

- Select one or two Category A-stressors that you are going to tackle now.
- Write down 3–5 action steps that you can take right away to start to tackle these one or two Category A-stressors.

For example, continuing with the example of wanting to move away from your small company and from Philadelphia, some action steps might include:

- Updating your resume
- Researching companies with a presence in your desired city
- Connecting with colleagues on LinkedIn
- Hiring a recruiter
- Brushing up on your interview skills with a course or seminar

WHAT YOU CAN EXPECT TO GAIN FROM THIS EXERCISE:

- What was a jumble of angst and fear is now unpacked and moved from your mind and onto your index cards. You have successfully taken the first step of the healing process.
- You have teased out the one or two Category A-stressors that are causing you to feel stuck, and you now have a mini-action plan to address them.

For me, just getting everything out of my head and into manageable pieces is liberating. If I can see it literally in front of me, I can then come up with a plan for the Category A "biggies" that involves manageable, actionable steps. Before you take any action, though, pause for a moment to consider how you feel seeing everything that has been weighing so heavily on your mind now unpacked and classified on your index cards. I hope you feel lighter. Do you feel like your fears and your stressors are starting to loosen their hold on you? By unbundling them, you can examine each one individually and prioritize what you are going to focus on to get unstuck and to move forward with your plan.

The reality is that some of our stressors are just not going to go away. And these can be significant, such as a chronic disease, the loss of a loved one, financial issues. For these, you should seek out help—from family, friends, spiritual counselors, or a therapist. I had to seek out the counsel of a therapist to help me work through a stressor in my life. She gave me a fresh perspective that brought great relief. Please do not try to carry these burdens of the heart alone.

Take action: Unpack your fears and stressors, make a plan, seek out the support you need.

As civil rights activist Rosa Parks said:

> “Knowing what must be done does away with fear.”

VOLTA AWAKENING

#4

CUTTING LOOSE YOUR ENERGY-DRAINERS

What people, places, or things are sucking the life out of you?

Over the years, I've had what I'll call an assortment of toxic elements in my professional life. They ran the gamut–bosses that were difficult to respect, negative office mates, and a few unsavory clients.

The point is this—it's inevitable. We're all going to encounter energy-drainers, and the longer we're in the workforce, the more of them we'll have to deal with.

Three times in my career I had an energy-drainer for a boss. All three were similar: They couldn't share the limelight, they never gave credit to their team, they couldn't make a decision, and they never stuck their neck out for anyone or anything. I found it to be very difficult to learn from this type of boss. Give me an unrelenting, crazed, hardcore, demanding boss, any day, over an insecure one. I want someone that I can learn from. I want a boss who will challenge me to bring my best–especially when they're bringing their best. Now that's something that I can respect.

Each time, I put together a plan of action to change my circumstances. One time I made a lateral move to another team, another time I interviewed and was promoted to another division, and the last time, I left the company to start a business. My point is this: Your boss is a pivotal person in your life—a boss is right up there with a life partner in terms of its "quality-of-life impact potential." Don't delay for too long when you have a lousy boss. Take action.

The same goes for clients. I *love* a tough client. They can be demanding, even snarky. I'm up for the challenge. And I will bring it. But if *they* are not bringing it, and they are regularly disrespectful, this becomes a situation that needs examining and action. When it looks like it's going to be a longer-term arrangement, you are going to want to make time for a courageous conversation with them. (More on that later.)

Then there's the negative, gossipy office mate. It's easy to get sucked in—you hear yourself chiming in with statements that you would *never* say to a person's face. I've been there. You wake up in the morning regretting what you said, and mad at yourself for getting pulled into the vortex. They're draining your enthusiasm for your company and for your career. It's contagious. This is not a healthy dynamic to operate under on a daily basis. And don't be fooled; it will have unintended consequences. Time to take a walk at lunch, stay away from the water cooler, move desks–whatever it takes. Just be sure to do something to nip it in the bud.

It's very important to identify and to address any energy-drainers and toxic elements in your professional life because they will bring you down–and life's too short for that.

Let's be specific about what I mean by an energy-drainer. It's a person, place or thing that has the potential to become an impediment to your success—such as the ones I have mentioned as well and others like, a company culture that doesn't align with your values, a geography that brings you down, a work environment where no one feels comfortable sharing their opinions, a "do *whatever* it takes to get the business" philosophy, a job that doesn't align with the fabric of your being, and being surrounded by people that aren't motivated to excel in their careers.

What I'm asking you to do is to answer this question for yourself: *What people, places, or things are sucking the life out of you?*

Energy-drainers are a fact of life. The trick is to take charge of them by either addressing them or by purposefully cutting them loose from your life.

Energy-drainers usually fall into two categories: what you can control and what you can't control. We have to learn to let go of what we can't control; however, I believe you'll discover that most of these energy-drainers can be addressed with awareness and a plan.

An energy-drainer does not inspire fear. Instead it feels like a constant drain of energy, a sense of hopelessness, or something that brings you down, even on a "good day." The energy-drainers in our life tend to be low-grade—this can lull us into thinking they will resolve on their own. Unfortunately, this is not something we can assume will happen. We need to tackle our energy-drainers head-on. *Think of this as an act of self-care.*

When we are faced with these toxic situations, things, or people, our gut instinct sends our brains signals to get our attention. The signals we receive can be things such as feeling like we are walking on eggshells, a feeling that we don't belong, a feeling of being manipulated, or maybe our entire perspective on our career life feels clouded. I once had a boss who was so scheming that my skin, from my feet to my head, literally crawled whenever I sat in her office. She had a very "charming" persona but I think she was actually a reptile.

WHO ARE YOUR 5 PEOPLE?

Have you heard Jim Rohn's quote: "We are the average of the five people we spend the most time with"? Who are *your* five people? Are they building you up or dragging you down?

Take a mental inventory of your five people and answer these questions for yourself:

- *Who should I spend more time with?*
- *Who should I spend less time with?*
- *Who should I stop spending time with?*

Remember—there are givers and takers. Be a giver, and surround yourself with other givers. For more information on this topic, I recommend that you read Adam Grant's book, *Give and Take: Why Helping Others Drives Our Success.*

CLEARING YOUR PATH

When our brain signals to us that our current situation is toxic, these signals are not to be ignored, because they are alerting us to unhealthy situations that have to be reckoned with. This is because, unresolved, these eventually become your *soul-killers,* a phrase I recently heard in journalist Megyn Kelly's interview with *Success* magazine.

EXERCISE #4:

IDENTIFYING YOUR ENERGY-DRAINERS

GETTING STARTED

- The first thing you are going to do is list, one per index card, the energy-drainer(s) in your professional life that you want to move away from—environments, or relationships that bring you down, or things that you are "sick of" or that make you cranky.
- Select your 2–3 biggest energy-drainers. Turn each one over and, on the back of the card, write down why you haven't yet initiated and completed the process of shutting the door on this disturbance in your life. Answer the questions: *What am I hoping for? What am I waiting for?*
- These roadblocks will require a "plan of elimination," so on the back of each card also write down 2–3 action steps that will serve to eliminate these elements from your professional life. This may mean a change of job, company, city, or relationship.

WHAT YOU CAN EXPECT TO GAIN FROM THIS EXERCISE:

- A concrete list of what you have to shed or move away from.
- Identification of the reasons why you haven't yet tackled the negative forces in your life that are roadblocks to your career aspirations.
- An awareness that it's time to take action—with your mini-elimination plan.

There will be times in life when the best solution will be for you to move on and away from a chronic toxic element in your life, be it a boss, a company, a culture, or a geography.

Take the advice of singer-songwriter Dolly Parton:

> "If you don't like the road you're walking on, start paving another one."

VOLTA AWAKENING

#5

SHAPING YOUR PERSONAL BRAND

How would others describe you as a brand?

Now that you are gaining enlightenment and an awareness of your inner self, it's time to take stock of what you are "putting out there"—your outer self.

The way you present yourself to others falls under your outer self—your persona, your personality. I am referring to how people *experience* you. We must try to "see" the version of ourselves that we are presenting to others. If we could watch a video of ourselves engaging at work in a typical week, we would realize that what we are projecting isn't always desirable, despite our best intentions.

This reminds me of another one of those very *influential times* in my career...

It happened approximately eight years after my partners and I had opened our doors for business. We were on top of the world: The business was growing at a rapid clip, and at the time, our top line was running around $40 million with a head-count of at least 125 employees. I attended a three-day seminar to strengthen my leadership skills. Weeks before arriving, we had to recruit 20 participants to fill out an online anonymous feedback survey. I asked the people that I worked with on a regular basis, and my two business partners, to provide their input.

The night before I left for the seminar, anxiety struck. It was then that I had a minute to consider what I had done–asking 20 people for their honest feedback is risky business. Especially when it's anonymous. We all know that under the veil of anonymity people let it rip. What the hell was I thinking? Hadn't I already earned my stripes and surpassed the need for any feedback at this juncture in my career?

On the second day of the seminar, each of us were handed a three-ring binder that was filled with charts, graphs, and numbers that captured and catalogued the feedback from our participants. As I turned each page and let the words and charts wash over me, I wanted to crawl under my chair. Yes, there was positive feedback but a couple of my scores were concerning. One of them was practically off the chart. That is, in a bad way, not in a good way. I glanced over at the three guys I had befriended at my table to see how they were holding up. Bob, an SVP of something, was in shock. The handsome Director of Anesthesiology was muttering "I'm going to fire the little f***ers." And Marty, the COO, said something like, "This seminar was useless."

Talk about a horribly enlightening way of getting feedback on what you're projecting. It was in black and white, with a few accent colors sprinkled in. It was impossible for me to unsee my charts. It took me a couple of months to fully appreciate the *gift* of this self-awareness. This feedback was directly related to me as a brand—so I had some work to do, especially because I wanted my team to feel *valued* and not micromanaged.

You will need to honestly answer this question for yourself: *How would others describe you as a brand?*

Make no mistake, you *are* a brand. Like Starbucks, Patagonia, Free People, BMW, and Apple, as people, we are *all* brands. When you stop and think about it, you're already shaping your brand with your Twitter, Facebook, and Instagram profiles.

Brands are designed with great care and purpose to make people feel a certain way. They are *experiential*. Successful brands command a higher price point. When it comes to a person-as-a-brand, this translates into a higher salary.

With this in mind, that you are a brand, if your coworkers, managers, and clients were to describe you as a brand, what might they say?

- What would they say are your great strengths?
- What would they say makes you unique?
- What would they say is your mission in life?

Are you more like:

- Ben & Jerry's or Häagen-Dazs?
- BMW or Subaru?
- Kohl's or Macy's?
- Starbucks or Dunkin' Donuts?
- American Express or Visa?

- iPhone or Android?
- Smartwater or Poland Spring?

When you think about yourself as a brand, you realize that you have the ability to make people feel something about you and, more importantly, you can directly impact how they feel about themselves.

As a brand, the people around you "experience" you, therefore it is essential to obtain self-awareness on two critical fronts, so you can understand what you need to reshape on behalf of your brand. You must gain self-awareness of:

- What you are **projecting** to others – your outward persona.
- How you are **connecting** with others – how you make people feel during their interactions with you.

I want to be ultra-clear about something. I'm not asking you to be a fake or a phony. I want you to be authentic. But I also want you to be the best version of you—someone who is aware of her impact. It's remarkable to me how many smart, motivated people *rarely pause* to contemplate their own behavior and the impact of their words and actions.

What we project and how we connect significantly affects how the people in our lives—the people who have the power to make or break our careers—are assessing us and our "promotability." Whether you realize it or not, and whether you like it or not, these individuals are making continuous assessments of you, both macro and micro, regarding career-impacting factors including:

- Can they envision you in a bigger role?
- How do you come across in meetings and social settings?
- What is your ability to influence a business outcome?

- What is your ability to rally a team around your company's mission?
- How will an important client feel when they interact with you?
- Are you committed, all-in?
- Can you be trusted?
- Do you care about yourself first or the team first?
- How do you handle tough conversations? Do you avoid them?
- How do you react in stressful business situations?
- Are you are catching or missing important "signals" that can have an impact on business?
- Can you inspire others?

That's quite a list, isn't it? Don't let it intimidate you—because I'm going to help you get your arms around where you, as a brand, stand in terms of what you are projecting and how you are connecting. I am going to introduce you to a few exercises to help you assess yourself as a brand, your *current self*. This will give you the baseline that you will need to build upon as you move from the reflection phase of this VOLTA process into the shaping of your *future self*. This will all come together in Part 3, where you will re-emerge as a better you—an even more promotable, more sought-after brand.

I've had the great pleasure of working side by side with some mega-brand builders. When these branding experts build a brand, they go through a disciplined process of making strategic selections of external elements such as a logo, color, tone, and visualization. These elements are carefully selected to foster the intended impact they want the brand to have on their target audience.

If we translate this work into the concept of a human as a brand, then we can appreciate how things like our body language, our presence, our voice, our communication style, and how we dress can have an impact on who we are as a brand—and how others might be experiencing us.

We need this self-awareness of the impact that we are having on people around us in the workplace because the fact is that—whether it's good or bad—we are having an effect on people. It's common for even the most well-intentioned people to come across in certain ways that could be off-putting: Perhaps you make people feel that you're not interested in them, or that you crave the spotlight, that you are defensive and can't handle feedback. Or maybe you're unknowingly giving off signals that you lack self-respect.

EXERCISE #5:

FIND OUT WHAT YOU ARE PROJECTING

Take some time to honestly answer these questions that are designed to illuminate what you might be projecting as you think about yourself on a typical day interacting with your colleagues. We will cover three topics: confidence, leadership, and off-putting behaviors. Rate yourself on the following charts, circling the number on a scale of 1 to 5.

ARE YOU PROJECTING CONFIDENCE?

These questions in the chart below will help to reveal:

- If you are a force to be taken seriously.
- If those on the receiving end experience a feeling that they are in good hands.

- If you are a woman who has done her homework.
- If you respect yourself, and if you are to be respected.
- If others get the sense that you are someone who isn't easily ignored.
- If you are someone who is warm and nonthreatening.

PROJECTING CONFIDENCE ASSESSMENT

DO YOU:	NEVER	ALMOST NEVER	SOMETIMES	ALMOST ALWAYS	ALWAYS
Enter a room with purpose?	1	2	3	4	5
Convey warmth?	1	2	3	4	5
Look into people's eyes?	1	2	3	4	5
Stand tall?	1	2	3	4	5
Deliberately occupy your space?	1	2	3	4	5
Have a firm handshake?	1	2	3	4	5
Bring forward an informed POV?	1	2	3	4	5
Ask informed questions?	1	2	3	4	5
Feel comfortable saying "no"?	1	2	3	4	5
Embrace self-compassion?	1	2	3	4	5
Have a curiosity-based mindset?	1	2	3	4	5

ARE YOU PROJECTING LEADERSHIP?

The questions in the chart below will help you to reveal:

- If you are a woman who assumes responsibility and is secure enough to give credit where credit is due.
- If your primary focus is on the team rather than yourself. If you believe that when the team wins, you win.
- If your leadership persona conveys that you are willing to have the tough conversations, to be imperfect, and to embrace the ups and downs in the workplace.

PROJECTING LEADERSHIP ASSESSMENT

DO YOU:	NEVER	ALMOST NEVER	SOMETIMES	ALMOST ALWAYS	ALWAYS
Paint a picture of the end goal?	1	2	3	4	5
Say "we" more than "I"?	1	2	3	4	5
Take responsibility for things?	1	2	3	4	5
Give credit to others?	1	2	3	4	5
Bring can-do solutions?	1	2	3	4	5
Bring calm to tense situations?	1	2	3	4	5
Have tough conversations?	1	2	3	4	5
Coach people on what needs to improve?	1	2	3	4	5
View setbacks as learnings?	1	2	3	4	5

ARE YOU PROJECTING SOMETHING OFF-PUTTING?

The questions in the chart below will help to reveal what you might unknowingly be doing that could be turning people off. These behaviors can make you come across as:

- Self-focused
- Prideful
- Closed-minded
- Defensive
- Insecure

Note: In this case, a high score is *not* what you're aiming for.

PROJECTING OFF-PUTTING BEHAVIORS ASSESSMENT

DO YOU:	NEVER	ALMOST NEVER	SOMETIMES	ALMOST ALWAYS	ALWAYS
Say "I" more than "we"?	1	2	3	4	5
Interrupt as people are explaining?	1	2	3	4	5
Use the word "but" when responding?	1	2	3	4	5
Debate to gain agreement?	1	2	3	4	5
Secretly need to be the smartest person in the room?	1	2	3	4	5
Convey closed-off body language?	1	2	3	4	5

DO YOU:	NEVER	ALMOST NEVER	SOMETIMES	ALMOST ALWAYS	ALWAYS
Come off as aggressive using your voice or body language?	1	2	3	4	5
Tend to assign blame?	1	2	3	4	5
Defend your position?	1	2	3	4	5
Believe it's easier to *just do it myself*?	1	2	3	4	5

EXERCISE #6:

FIND OUT HOW YOU ARE CONNECTING WITH OTHERS

The second critical area relates to how you are connecting with others. The strongest, most successful "brands":

- Connect in a felt and meaningful way with the people around them.
- Demonstrate true interest in people and their opinions.
- Create an environment where people can feel good about themselves.

Take some time to honestly answer these questions that are designed to illuminate how well you are connecting with others as you think about yourself on a typical day interacting with your colleagues.

CONNECTING WITH OTHERS ASSESSMENT

DO YOU:	NEVER	ALMOST NEVER	SOMETIMES	ALMOST ALWAYS	ALWAYS
Actively listen to what is being said?	1	2	3	4	5
Listen to what is *not* being said?	1	2	3	4	5
Take note of others' body language?	1	2	3	4	5
Seek out common ground?	1	2	3	4	5
Put yourself in other people's shoes?	1	2	3	4	5
Leverage questions as a way to connect on a deeper level?	1	2	3	4	5
Let people save face when they make a mistake?	1	2	3	4	5
Leverage humor to lighten the mood?	1	2	3	4	5
Convey a relaxing aura through your body language?	1	2	3	4	5
Believe that people are trying to do their best?	1	2	3	4	5

You've done some hard work assessing yourself, but all that effort will come to fruition in Part 3—where we will weave your self-awareness learnings into your VOLTA Career Plan.

I highly recommend that you ask three or so of the people you interact with on the job to give you an honest score to each of these questions. This feedback can bring a lot of additional value when included with your own self-assessments. **Note:** There is a copy of each of these assessment charts in the Appendix of this book. You may also sign up on our website to receive a PDF version of these assessment charts–www.voltalife.org.

Whether or not we recognize it, we connect with others through our behavior. You need to be fully aware of this: Is what you are projecting drawing your colleagues in—or pushing them away? Is yours a brand others seek out? Is yours a brand that is viewed as a confident, promotable leader? Is yours a brand that allows for both your fun side and your professional side to live together in harmony?

As we close out this section on you as a brand, I'd like you to reflect on the words of author Jan Fields:

> "You build your personal brand through everything you do, whether by action or small decisions, and the brand will stay with you throughout your career."

Be very mindful of your brand. Shape it intentionally and authentically with your heart and soul.

READY TO TURN TO PART 2

It's now time for you to harness the power of all of your self-discoveries and move on to Part 2. There you will find the 5 VOLTA Trade Secrets—the best practices of successful women—all in one place. This will arm you with the wisdom, and the methods and techniques, you will need in Part 3 to map out your VOLTA Career Plan and ignite your career power.

PART 2

YOUR 5 VOLTA TRADE SECRETS

THE INDISPENSABLE MUST-HAVES FOR CAREER SUCCESS

“…to learn

and learn again

from those

who know.”

FROM *ITHACA*
BY C.P. CAVAFY

YOU ARE MOVING FULL STEAM AHEAD to the VOLTA change-point in your career life. You now have a deeper understanding of your mindset, your inner voice, your fears and stressors, and your energy-drainers. You now have more clarity with respect to knowing yourself as a brand.

Sit in a little closer, because I'm going to share with you proven trade secrets that separate the winners from the losers in the workplace. They are the "best practices" I have curated for you with one driving focus in mind: **To get you noticed and to get you on the fastest path to career success.**

What it boils down to is this: There are 5 Trade Secrets that are the lynchpin to greater promotability and career success. These 5 Trade Secrets leverage my firsthand experience and weave it together with the collective wisdom of prominent career women from multiple industries who know how to get noticed and make an impact. These 5 Trade Secrets will provide the how-tos that will give you the competitive edge to rise above the pack and advance at a significantly faster pace. Remember this: It's all about the *nuances*.

THE 5 VOLTA TRADE SECRETS:

#1 How to bolster your GRAVITAS
#2 How to earn your seat at The Table
#3 How to have Courageous Conversations
#4 How to Unlearn and Lead
#5 How to strengthen your Moxie Muscle

At the beginning of each of the 5 Trade Secrets chapters, I will define and describe each trade secret and I will invite you to score yourself on a scale of 1-10. Then we will take a deep dive into the how-tos of each trade secret where I will give lots of practical advice and methods that you can put into practice right away on your VOLTA journey.

Let's get started!

VOLTA TRADE SECRET

#1

HOW TO BOLSTER YOUR GRAVITAS

GRAVITAS is the motherload.

From the age of say 13 to 32, I frequently shrank back, trying to be small, flying under the radar. Some of it was collateral damage from my parents' divorce. I felt a deep unworthiness, of being *less than* other people. I had several years of internal wincing, feeling ugly, and being socially awkward. I pushed myself through most of these situations, but it was *definitely a push*. I wasn't really comfortable with "being me" at all.

I had a turning point, a VOLTA, when Meredith was born. During her 2 a.m. feedings, while on maternity leave, I would get upset thinking about all of the things that happened to me at work during my pregnancy—most significantly the humiliation in my first Marketing position that came with my demotion to a smaller brand. Poor Meredith. Let's just say that sometimes the 2 a.m. "burping" that she got from me wasn't exactly delicate patting.

It was during those six weeks that I took stock each night and made the decision to make the necessary changes—to deliberately evolve into a stronger version of me. Burchard talks about the power of doing something out of "necessity" in his book *High Performance Habits*. For me, I *needed* to be a strong role model for Meredith. It was instinctual. It was born out of my deep maternal love and desire to be the best mother I could be for *her*. And so it began, at the age of 32, my journey to GRAVITAS. It felt like a late start, but it was a start.

My road to GRAVITAS was a journey of learning and practice. I learned that when you have GRAVITAS, you can feel it and *they* can feel it. That it's both physical and psychological. Psychologically you're 100% grounded in your being. You know who you are and you're good with it. Physically, I can really feel it when I'm standing. I feel anchored to the floor like a large boulder. No one can knock me down or push me around. Good luck trying.

I've learned to be comfortable in my skin, to truly like myself, and I redirect, as needed, my inner dialogue to be affirming and friendly. (Our inner dialogue plays such a crucial role in having GRAVITAS.)

I practiced and learned that I'm absolutely fine with not being perfect. I talk freely about my struggles. People seem to like hearing about something that you're struggling with—it makes you human. No one is perfect–and perfect is a big yawn anyway.

I learned, practiced, and mastered being acutely *other-focused.* I am deeply interested in what other people have to say. I take note of the color of their eyes. I notice if their hands are shaking, even the slightest tremor. Do they have any nervous hives on their neck? I notice pretty much everything.

And I've done my homework. By God, I've done my homework. This gives me the permission to speak out and to ask well-informed questions.

There's a warm and humble side to GRAVITAS, too.

I'm intentionally welcoming. I am an encourager–I want people to shine. I forgive and I ask to be forgiven. And I pray for humility.

As I think about it, if I had to choose to do only one thing in my life, it would be coaching career women to discover and cultivate their GRAVITAS (*GRA•vi•taz*). I love the word GRAVITAS because it's one of those words that sounds like what it means—substance, weightiness, and power. GRAVITAS is a crucial ingredient for *presence* because when you have it, people know it. People feel it. When they feel your personal power, they will respect you and they will take you seriously.

You can take my position, you can take my clients, you can take my business—but you can't take my GRAVITAS. With my GRAVITAS, I will reboot, rebuild, and return—even stronger.

GRAVITAS is a state of mind—and it's a state of being. It takes a deliberate, conscious effort. If you're willing to make the effort, then you can absolutely work your way to becoming a woman with GRAVITAS. That's exactly how I did it. It was deliberate. It took lots of practice. It required humility. It was 100% learned.

It's important for you to be fully aware of the things you are doing, or not doing, that have an impact on your GRAVITAS. Projecting *I've got this* and *I deserve to be here* denotes your certainty about your value.

Know that you are continually being assessed at work. Make no mistake, in the workplace you need to be in your "on-mode." The workplace is not the place to let down your hair. It's not the place to "wing it." From your day-to-day routines to your client-facing engagements, you are representing not only your personal brand, but also your company's brand and your clients' brands. Your managers are taking note of the influence you have within the walls of your company—this lets them envision how it will translate in work situations that are beyond those walls. Think of it this way—you are an extension of your manager, and you are a representative of your company. Therefore, you must always be aware of your presence—that's one of the realities of the work environment.

Without GRAVITAS, you are likely to be overlooked. This does not have to be the case. With awareness, with practice, and with purpose, **having GRAVITAS is definitely within every career woman's reach.**

Here's what a woman with GRAVITAS looks like, sounds like, and feels like:

- She exudes confidence
- She has a voice that conveys authority and carries weight
- She has a strong, warm presence
- She has the composure to be still and silent when appropriate
- She has the power to influence decisions
- She has an ability to speak the truth—even when it's unpopular

All of these elements, when combined, culminate into a career woman who has GRAVITAS—she is valued, she is trusted, she commands respect. And please don't buy into the belief that you're too young or "too junior" to have it. GRAVITAS is like trustworthiness—every woman can, and should, have it.

Your career will catapult when you commit to cultivating your GRAVITAS.

Assess your GRAVITAS with the GRAVITAS-Meter

Take a look at the self-assessment scale that follows, and circle your current level of GRAVITAS. (Don't worry if it's not where you'd like it to be—we're going to change that!)

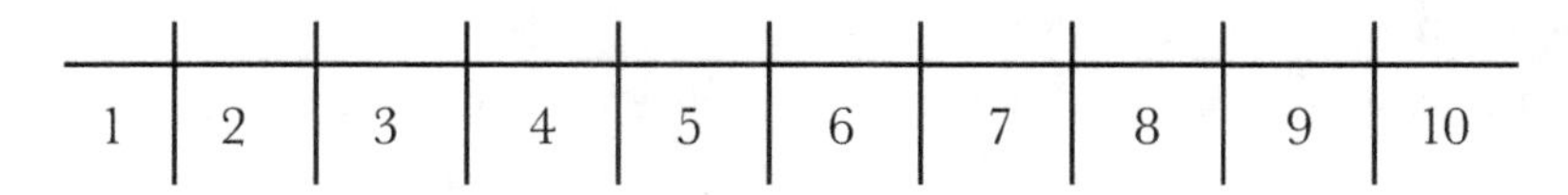

What's GRAVITAS? Average More than most I've got this!

GRAVITAS VS. POISE VS. SCRAPPINESS

I've heard the word "poised" used to describe certain women, and I've also heard people use the word "scrappy." We are going to examine the difference between a woman with GRAVITAS vs. one who is poised or scrappy. *Poise* is defined as being dignified and self-composed. *Scrappy* is having a determined spirit, being resourceful, and feisty.

Is it a compliment to be referred to as scrappy? Personally, I would rather *not* have you described as being scrappy. As for poise, it's a great start, but not everyone described as "poised" can claim to influence people and drive decisions.

My goal for you: For people to see and feel your GRAVITAS—because it is the recognizable culmination of so many things that are critical to advancing in the business world.

Let's take a look at a direct comparison between scrappiness, poise, and GRAVITAS in the following chart. You will notice that each category has some elements in common, like commitment and doing your homework. However, after that, the similarities between these three styles start to diverge.

SCRAPPY	POISE	GRAVITAS
• Well-informed	• Well-informed	• Well-informed
• Does her homework	• Does her homework	• Does her homework
• Committed	• Committed	• Committed
• Inwardly focused	• Outwardly focused • Engaging	• Outwardly focused • Engaging • Makes others feel welcomed and important
• Nervous energy	• Self-composed	• Self-composed • Exudes confidence
• Minimal eye contact, perhaps even darting eyes	• Good eye contact	• Purposeful eye contact • Her eyes convey that she's listening
• Not really listening; she's frequently thinking about what she's going to say next	• Good listener • People feel heard	• Listens with purpose • People feel heard • She is soaking in her surroundings for important cues

SCRAPPY	POISE	GRAVITAS
• Body movements can be a distraction because of her nervous energy	• Purposeful body movements	• Purposeful body movements • Purposefully occupies space • Enters the room with confidence
• Her voice can be pitchy or timid	• Voice is credible	• Voice is credible • Voice is declarative
• Her handshake is infrequent and rather weak	• A firm handshake is common practice	• A firm handshake is a must-have • Her purposeful eye contact says "Welcome" and "I'm happy that we met"

I hope you notice that scrappiness does align on a few elements, but it quickly diverges to a path of, let's call it, "nervous energy." Poise aligns with GRAVITAS for several key categories such as composure, listening, eye contact, and purposeful body movements. But even poise and GRAVITAS eventually diverge because GRAVITAS brings even more. It's all about the nuances—it's the nuances that make all the difference between someone who is comfortable in her skin vs. a powerbroker who influences decisions and commands a room with her warm charisma.

I have to admit something that I realized as I was writing this. I used to be scrappy! No wonder that word strikes such a negative chord with me. I was determined, resourceful, and I worked my butt off. There were lots of late nights, long hours—your basic blood, sweat, and tears. Yet I was overlooked and not taken seriously. And considering all of the effort that I had invested, why weren't things clicking? It's because, at the time, I was probably more like a spirited Jack Russell terrier and not a woman projecting GRAVITAS.

Everything–from the way we hold ourselves to the way we dress, to how we enter a room, to the firmness of our handshake and whether we establish eye contact, to the way we sit and stand, and project our voice—reveals the value we place on our personal brand.

Do you make others feel that they are in good hands? Are you conveying that you belong, that you are a trusted source to be taken seriously? I will make sure that you have everything you need to be that confident woman whom others notice, admire, and promote.

We're going to do this in a way that you will be seen as a contender but *not* in a way that makes you lose what makes you, *you*. There will be things that you will have to adjust, but not over-adjust, because I want you to be an authentic, enhanced version of you. You can acquire your own personal brand of GRAVITAS by embracing these five proven practices.

DRESS TO SAY "I'VE GOT THIS"

Deciding what to wear is probably the first of many decisions you will make each day, and this is the one most capable of making you feel prepared and ready to go—*wearing* your GRAVITAS. I'm a big believer in dressing in a way that projects confidence. My go-to confidence booster is the sharply tailored jacket. For some women, it's a pair of heels or a signature color. Even a statement piece of jewelry. Whatever gives you confidence and makes you aware that *you are a force* is what you should wear. Flats aren't something I choose to wear in more formal business settings.

When you're only 5'3", like me, why would you? Yes, you should feel comfortable in your own skin, but when it comes to your career, you need to remain mindful of your presence, and what you choose to wear makes an immediate impression. The well-cut suit jacket, even paired with jeans, *projects strength.*

And who doesn't want to feel stronger? Find what works for you and work it. If you're unsure, ask a trusted friend or invest in a few hours of a stylist's expertise. Your mission is to dress like a woman who knows—and projects—her value. She is polished and put-together. We may not be as tall or as slim as we would like, but looking polished and put-together is a requirement and very doable.

MASTER THE ALL-IMPORTANT HANDSHAKE

Perhaps no other gesture so clearly makes an immediate impression as the handshake. Done well, with firmness and warmth, it communicates so much that words cannot. It says: *Hello. Welcome. I want to be here. I'm delighted that you're here. Let's collaborate.* My friend refers to this kind of handshake as a "hand-hug."

On the other hand, a weak, limp handshake communicates a lack of interest and says, *I'm not a contender. Don't take me seriously.*

When you give a strong, firm (non-sweaty) handshake—with deep and caring eye contact—it will make the other person feel like they are the most important person in the room, all while allowing your GRAVITAS to shine. Giving a weak handshake, with all that it communicates, is, quite frankly, inexcusable and unflattering, especially for you.

After reading this, my daughter Meredith asked me to assess her handshake. She thought hers was good and firm. It wasn't. I had her try three times, each time adding more strength. Finally, she nailed it. Ladies, her new handshake has *triple* the original firmness. And I don't mean bone-crushing power. I mean the kind of firmness that made me, the recipient, feel good—and it conveyed Meredith's confidence and strength.

How do *you* know if you have a good, firm handshake? Find a pal and practice. I would say, as a general rule, double down on your firmness. Going forward, walk into a room with purpose and extend your hand to everyone as a warm, welcoming gesture. A confident handshake will now become one of your hallmarks.

P.S. I have to mention this because it's happened to me a few times over the years... There will be times when you misfire—when your hand and theirs don't quite connect properly. We've all had some misfires, but there's no shame in laughing and saying, "Let's try that again!"

If you find yourself walking into a room that has a mix of clients or business associates *and* team members, what I find that works best is to shake the hands of the clients and associates and say a warm "hello" to each person on your team.

CONNECT WITH WARM EYE CONTACT AND MEANINGFUL QUESTIONS

The eyes don't lie. In the past few years, I have come to recognize the power of warm eye contact. I am now fully appreciating just how *deeply connecting warm eye contact* can be. But I struggled for a long time to make this connecting eye contact in business settings. I felt exposed and a bit vulnerable. Now I'm finding, more so than a hug, purposeful and caring eye contact works on several important levels. It connotes a desire to connect as a fellow human being, and it demonstrates calmness and confidence. Engaging in warm eye contact, for me, has had a 100% positive response rate.

In contrast, a lack of eye contact, or, even worse, darting eyes, communicates nervousness and a lack of interest in the other person—the exact *opposite* of GRAVITAS. I am someone who tends to be more introverted when meeting people for the first time or in unfamiliar situations, but the time came for me to **get over myself.** The good news is that you can work at establishing these deeper connections. For example: Plan ahead for that client dinner, and tell yourself that you will meet and genuinely interact with three new people—by leveraging eye contact and by asking meaningful questions about them. Preplanning with the help of LinkedIn and other readily available resources is a valuable strategy for these business settings. I guarantee that you will be pleasantly surprised at how receptive people will be to this form of engagement.

I was recently told that I was "radiant" in a social gathering. This compliment was very meaningful to me because it's something that I'd never been told before and because it was born out of something that I had to learn and practice doing—an intentional pushing through my introverted nature. The funny thing is that I didn't do much talking that evening at all—I simply asked everyone I spoke with a couple of genuine, I'm-interested-in-you questions and then listened with deep interest and made warm eye contact as they shared themselves with me.

Here's the thing: Putting *others* in the spotlight actually creates a glow around *you*. It's time to turn that self-critical lens away from yourself. The more you can get into this "it's-not-about-me mode," so much about life and people will be illuminated—and you will be radiant!

SPEAK WITH A DECLARATIVE VOICE

Your voice is one of the most powerful tools that can project GRAVITAS. It simply cannot be ignored, especially if you don't want others to ignore you. Your voice is one of the most important indicators of confidence or the lack of confidence. If your voice is too soft, or if you have an affectation such as "upspeak" (an upward pitch at the end of a declarative sentence) or "vocal fry" (drawing out the end of a sentence with a low, croaky voice), this requires immediate attention.

These vocal affectations can make you come across as tentative and unsure. This will detract from the message that you are communicating. You want the opposite dynamic in your work-related dealings. You want your message to be heard. You want to project confidence and assuredness.

If you're lucky enough to have been gifted with a naturally strong speaking voice, leverage the hell out of it. If you *do* have a naturally strong voice, chances are you will have heard this compliment by now. Unfortunately, if you have a pitchy or weak voice, I doubt anyone has had the guts to tell you this. So you will have to ask for this specific feedback. My advice is to ask a few people, who hear you speak in work-related settings, their thoughts on your speaking voice. Ask if your voice projects confidence. Ask if it sounds weak or pitchy.

In a recent study led by Duke University that made headlines on CBS and in the *Washington Post* and *TIME*, it was revealed that vocal fry was a significant detractor—it made women and men with this affectation sound "less competent," "less educated," and "less hirable."

Do you end your sentences on an up note or a down beat? You should always be declarative—that is, to end your sentences with clarity and conviction. In my experience, many women end their sentences on an up note, which conveys asking about something vs. making a point or having an opinion about something. Don't lift your voice at the end of your sentences. **Visualize your sentences ending with a period,** not with a question mark.

Here's the good news about your voice: It can absolutely improve with practice. But, it has to be tended to. Record yourself and listen to how you sound; practice in front of a mirror. If you need to improve your speaking voice, and you're serious about getting to that next level in your career, invest in a short course of voice-coaching sessions.

Get yourself a copy of *It's the Way You Say It* by Carol Fleming. It's a great resource with lots of pointers for honing your speaking voice.

MOVE WITH PURPOSE...AND OCCUPY SOME SPACE

Do you enter a room with purpose? Does your posture convey confidence? When you walk into a room in a way that puts others at ease, when you set your mindset to receptivity and a curiosity to learn, when you bring positive energy, you become a source of sparkle. This kind of presence is contagious. Set your inner dialogue to: *I'm happy to be with you and I look forward to learning from you.* In doing so, others will feel welcomed and respected—and you will be a key contributor to a vibe of collaboration and trust. Most importantly, your presence will be noticed and your warm GRAVITAS will be felt.

PURPOSE + PRESENCE + WARMTH = GRAVITAS

I'm about to share some very specific techniques to help you build your personal power. These techniques will probably feel a bit unnatural at first. That's okay. With time and practice, they will become second nature for you. They did for me and the women I've coached. These techniques will put others at ease and will convey *I've got this.* I will address the way you stand, the way you enter a room, and the way you sit. For example, the next time you sit at a table in a work environment, take note of what you do:

When you're **sitting:**

- Are your hands on the table or underneath it?
- Are you deliberately taking up space, or are you making yourself small, hoping to go unnoticed?
- How is your posture? Are your shoulders slumped? Are they up at your ears? Or are they in a down and comfortable position?

Here's what good looks like when you are **sitting** at a conference table:

- Place your palms down on the table and rest them shoulder-width apart, purposely and comfortably occupying your space. Don't try to be small. Don't put your hands under the table. Sit back in your chair just a little, but lean in as necessary to express interest.

- If you are the leader at the table, it's your job to put your team at ease. Some ways to do this include placing an arm on the back of the chair, crossing your legs, and sitting a bit back from the table.
- No matter where you are in your career, you need to purposely occupy some space, and your internal dialogue should run along the lines of: *I'm confident, I'm ready,* and *This is going to be interesting!*

When you're **standing:**

- Are your legs crossed?
- Are you slumping or rocking back and forth?
- Is your stance or posture suggesting: I am weak or I am unworthy?

Here's what good looks like when you are *standing* in a work-related setting:

- Stand with your feet shoulder-width apart. Deliberately feel the bottoms of your feet firmly grounded to the floor. Don't rock. Relax your shoulders. Purposefully occupy your space. Don't try to be small. It may feel somewhat exaggerated at first, but I guarantee you will feel grounded. You will convey an aura of strength—strength of body and strength of mind.
- If crossing your arms makes you feel comfortable, that's okay, but if you're having a difficult conversation, be aware that this body language may read as defensive. So exercise judgment.
- Practice the stance that makes you feel comfortable and confident, and set your inner dialogue to: *I've done my homework* and *I'm happy to participate* and *I'm prepared for this conversation.*

There are two books I thoroughly enjoyed reading that take a deeper dive into many of the topics we've been discussing—purposeful movement, body language, and human connection. They are: *Executive Presence* by Sylvia Ann Hewlett and *Captivate* by Vanessa Van Edwards.

We have discussed and described in great detail what GRAVITAS—a powerful presence—looks and feels like. Now we must talk about those 10 things that you might be doing, most likely unknowingly, that can detract from or even undermine your power base. I refer to these as the "power-robbers." Women do them—men, as a general rule, don't.

THE 10 GRAVITAS POWER-ROBBERS

Power-robbers make me crazy! You need to be very aware of them, pay close attention to which ones you do, and then make it your business to scrub them out of your personal brand, today. Here's the list. Read it and be honest with yourself. What are you doing in a workplace setting that might be eroding your GRAVITAS?

- Do you make yourself small, trying to fade back into your surroundings?
- Do you have a weak, limp handshake?
- Is your physicality or how you dress suggesting, *Don't take me seriously*?
- Do you tilt your head to one side when listening? (This could be read as submissiveness.)
- Do you fiddle with or twirl your hair? (These kinds of "tics" could convey a lack of confidence.)
- Do you nod your head up and down listening to someone speak when you disagree with them?! Are you comfort-

able with moments of silence during a conversation, or do you fill them with nervous chatter?

- Does your voice have affectations? Is it pitchy? Do you have vocal fry? Are you ending sentences with a question mark?
- Do you avoid eye contact?
- Is your lens on the world turned toward yourself in *self-critic* mode?

GRAVITAS VOLTA MOMENTS

Use the lines below to reflect on whether you've had any illuminations regarding:

- Your presence
- Your purposeful approach to occupy your space
- Your clothing choices
- Your handshake
- Your eye contact
- Your speaking voice
- Your effort to engage with caring questions

ACTIONS

Declare below what you will start doing right away to enhance your GRAVITAS:

____

____

____

____

____

VOLTA TRADE SECRET

#2

HOW TO EARN YOUR SEAT AT THE TABLE

Your seat at The Table has to be earned. And don't kid yourself...it takes hard work.

In the Introduction of this book I shared the story about my first career VOLTA. I was finally at The Table but I wasn't prepared to be there. I vowed to never let that happen to me again.

Since that fateful day, I have lived by the adage "knowledge is power" and I'm *always* at-the-ready to sit at The Table...

One time when I was an SVP with FCB, I was asked to *listen in* on a meeting to gain an insider's understanding of an emerging new strategy with our largest client. My client said that all I needed to do was to bring printouts of the most recent version of the launch campaign. "Easy peasy" as my sister Leah would say.

It was going to be such a treat to be able to sit back and *take things in* instead of my usual role of presenting and being "on." When the day came, I settled into a fine-smelling leather chair in one of their formal conference rooms. I plucked a chewy little peanut butter candy from the crystal bowl perched in front of me. It was a Mary Jane, a taffy-type candy. I thought to myself, *How lovely, I haven't had one of these in years!*

My client started the meeting right on time. I noticed that there were quite a few senior-level people in the room. Other than the bright red blotches that were spreading across my client's neck, all seemed fine. I quietly unwrapped the Mary Jane and popped it into my mouth as she opened the meeting. Then I sat back to listen. Next thing I knew, she looked my way in a panic. She said my name and then she tossed the meeting over to me! Change of plans, people. It was going to be *me* making the presentation today. Other than the fact that taffy was stuck to my molars, I was ready. I shoved the remaining blob of candy under my tongue, sat forward and proceeded to lead the meeting. (It still makes me chuckle, every time I remember that day.)

Bottom line: To earn and to keep our seat at The Table, we *always* have to be prepared and in *on-mode.*

When you are invited to The Table, this is your chance to be recognized as a source of value by the decision-makers, so make sure you are ultra-prepared.

Much like GRAVITAS, earning your seat at The Table begins with your mindset and your inner dialogue. To be viewed as a contender at The Table, set your inner dialogue to: *I belong here.* And set your mindset to *curious learner.* In addition to having the right inner dialogue and the right mindset, it is vital that you *come prepared.* Because if you don't, you can bet the farm on this—it will be noticed.

Here's something else to digest as you think about earning your seat at The Table...

In life, the sooner you push yourself to do something challenging, the more natural it will become. This holds true for being at The Table. The sooner you hold the belief that you belong at The Table, the better. Start getting comfortable with the idea of being at The Table right now. Don't allow self-defeating habits of thinking and doing get etched any deeper into your psyche.

Here's what it looks like when a woman has earned her seat at The Table:

- She truly believes that knowledge is power—she has done her homework, and she has a well-informed point of view.
- She thinks like an owner—she deliberately considers the bigger picture, beyond her current role and responsibilities.
- She is an active participant who brings value—she knows when to speak up, and when to just listen.

When you commit to learning everything you can and bring it to The Table, your career gets the boost it needs—and you will launch ahead of the pack.

Assess how you fill your seat with the Earn-Your-Seat-at-The-Table-Meter

Take a look at the self-assessment scale that follows, and circle where you are in the process of earning your seat at The Table. (Be honest with yourself—it's very doable to get better at this!)

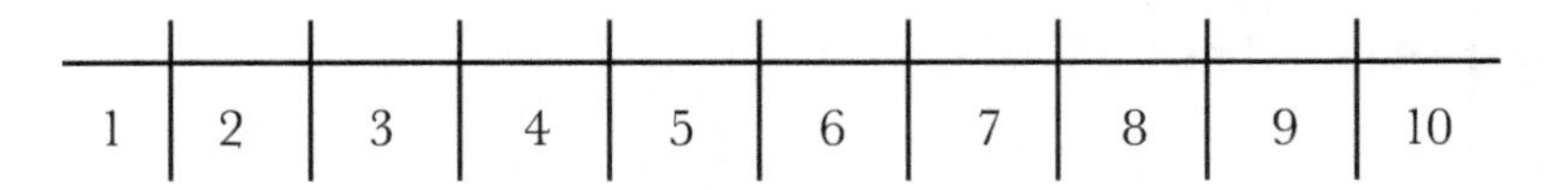

Just starting out Getting better Holding my own Rockin' it

There are seven essential components of earning your seat at The Table that will set you apart and accelerate you along the promotion track:

- Living by the words "knowledge is power"
- Thinking like an owner
- Bringing forward an idea
- Answering and asking questions
- Disagreeing with someone
- Listening with your ears...and your eyes
- Providing a briefing

LIVING BY THE WORDS "KNOWLEDGE IS POWER"

What if I told you there is one simple action you could be doing—that most of your "competition" is not doing—that will propel you forward in your career?

This simple action is to take 15–30 minutes of your day, each day, to immerse yourself in your industry, your company's industry, and your client's industry. I refer to these daily readings as "power sessions." During these power sessions, you will unearth and discover invaluable insights about your industry, your competition, your customers, and the overall landscape that impacts the ability to grow sales and market share. And if you are in the not-for-profit sector, this enhanced awareness will make it much easier for your company to rally people to take action and align with the mission of the organization.

Most importantly, this easy and highly impactful investment of your time will let you replace the "small talk" with something energizing and meaningful to discuss with your senior management—and with your clients. This will give you clout. Clout gives you the ability to directly impact decisions. When you put this all together, you're on your way to "commanding the room."

As Francis Bacon wrote 400 years ago—and it definitely holds true today:

> "Knowledge is power."

Knowledge is the *wow factor* that empowers people to achieve great results. The more knowledge a woman gains, the more powerful she becomes. This is crucial in any industry—the more you learn about who and what you are dealing with, the more of a force you will become.

Staying well-informed is a daily endeavor that requires both diligence and enthusiasm. For me, collecting insights and nuggets of wisdom is a personally rewarding practice, but make no mistake: I also make this a daily habit because of the value it brings to me as a career woman. For years, I have relied on these daily power sessions to *set me apart*. The important thing is to keep learning and assimilating information. And yes, it's hard work. Standing out among your competition and being successful is hard work. But, in the end, the hard work will definitely pay off!

"How do I do this? What should I read?"

All of us have, at our fingertips, access to an unprecedented goldmine of well-established online and offline resources. To name a few, there are: market research reports, blogs, websites, press releases, and podcasts. Your Twitter and Pinterest feeds can also serve as a good source of industry-related content. This is the day and age of equal access to every possible type of information that will make us highly informed knowledge sources within our industry. If you aren't sure about the best sources in *your* industry, ask your manager...ask your client. Then sign up. There really is no excuse.

You will get so much more out of these 15–30-minute daily power sessions if you ask yourself these key questions as you're scanning your resources:

- How could this information help or hurt my company/brand/service?
- How can we use this knowledge to destabilize the competition?
- How can we leverage this information to grow awareness, revenue, market share?
- What can we do with this new insight to change the thinking of our customers in a way that's favorable to our company/brand/service?
- How can I use this new knowledge to further differentiate and bolster the growth of my company/brand/service?

Another powerful method that will get you invited to The Table with your senior leadership and your clients is to purposely *get into their heads.* Here are some questions to ask yourself that will guide that process:

- What issues are likely to be keeping them up at night? How can I help with that?
- What do they probably need to be successful in their job? How can I help with that?
- How do they define success?
- What are their career goals? How can I help them achieve them?
- Are there any organizational politics, sensitive subjects, for me to be mindful of?

Anyone who doesn't take the time to be prepared is unwittingly holding themselves back from getting ahead. Don't kid yourself—if you're not in the know, you *will* be found out. Maybe not the first time, but after two or three times it's very likely that you will be thought of as something unflattering. I have heard phrases like *underwhelming, empty suit, blowhard, casual, lightweight,* and someone who *wings it.* Remember, people are always taking note of the value you bring. This is something that's totally in your hands, so do your homework, and become known as a go-to source of value!

Note: If you find that you don't enjoy digging into the details of your industry, this may be a sign that you've landed in an industry that doesn't align with your interests.

On the other hand, if you *are* doing what you want to be doing, in an industry that jazzes you, and you've been winging it—stop now! You need to find the time—make the time—to gain the necessary knowledge because when you do, your senior management and your clients will think wonderful things about you. They'll probably never say these things to you, but I can guarantee you that they will be thinking: *She makes me look good* and *Thank goodness she's on the team.*

THINKING LIKE AN OWNER

There is *always* a bigger picture. What lies beyond your role and responsibilities—beyond your position or team or department or division—forms a far larger representation of the industry you are a part of. Recognizing this helps you to identify threats and opportunities, while allowing you to plan for them like an owner would—with the best interests of the company in mind. When you sweep all of this into your thinking, you are considering the *whole system* and not just your specific part in it. This way of thinking will make you poised to bring recommendations and solutions that stand out. Your big-picture outlook will set you apart from the others whose focus is more limited...in the weeds.

When you seek out and frame things in the bigger picture—*what's best for the company*—you will be a stand-out. This kind of thinking also means that you will be trusted. Trusted that your interest is not self-serving, and that you're not out to protect your position or department above all else. Trusted that you have considered other points of view and that multiple angles have been examined. Trusted that your decisions don't need to be second-guessed. Plain and simple, your references to the big picture will instill confidence in others...and get you noticed.

Here are some questions to ask yourself that will put you in a "think like an owner" mindset:

- What is the primary vision/mission of our company?
- What are this year's key objectives?

- What's on the horizon that's either a threat or an opportunity?
- What struggles are we currently facing as a company?
- What do we fear?
- What's happening with our competitors?
- How can I help to improve our top-line growth?
- How can I help to improve our bottom-line savings?

BRINGING FORWARD AN IDEA

When you've done your homework, you are in a position to have a point of view (POV) that will add value to the discussion and the decisions that are made at The Table. I believe and respect the concept of quiet power; however, if you aren't an *engaged* participant at The Table, it will be noticed. Perhaps it's the "opener" that's holding you back—the words you use to set up and share your views and your thinking on a given topic. Typical interjections will usually be in the service of starting a topic, or adding to and expanding a topic stream.

Next time you're at The Table and you want to bring forward your perspective, try out some of my favorite go-to openers:

- "Here's something for us to consider..."
- "I recently read something that could have an impact on our industry..."
- "Imagine if..."
- "Lately our customers have been saying..."
- "To add to what Leslee said..."

Please don't make the mistake that too many women make—that is to start out with something apologetic, like:

- "This might sound stupid, but..."
- "I'm not sure if this matters, but..."

Also, don't fall into the trap of repeating (even if you change the wording a little) what someone already said. It's annoying as hell and eventually you will be thought of as a "repeater" who doesn't bring a perspective of her own.

ANSWERING AND ASKING QUESTIONS

Answering questions:
I learned early in my career that I would have to know my stuff and be ready to field all questions. It's unrealistic to expect that you could possibly have all the answers, but if you are asked a question that you don't have all the information to answer as completely as you would like—you should *not* reply with a general "I don't know."

You may have been counseled to say, "I don't know, but I'll find out." However, to my ears, it is much more impressive to respond with: "Here's what I *do* know..."

I can guarantee that you will know *something* about the topic. This will establish that you are informed and aware, then others will trust that you'll make it your business to search out a more complete answer and get back to them.

Asking questions:
People don't ask enough questions. A recent book, *Ask More,* by Frank Sesno, reports that as children we ask up to 500 questions a day. This number nosedives as we mature. It seems that as adults we no longer take advantage of the success that asking questions can bring. It should come as no surprise to you, then, that **the best leaders ask the best questions**. Well-crafted questions extract the details that provide the best informa-

tion—the most illuminating insights—that can guide your plan of action to profoundly better solutions.

It's true that asking questions requires courage...because we're not always prepared for the answer. There's a risk in every question, in that you might not like the response—or that you're not going to have an answer on the spot—but isn't it better to be informed and to know what someone's really thinking than not?

There's an art to framing questions. Questions should be framed to invite information, and not be framed in a way that is unintentionally accusatory, challenging, or intimidating. You should be clear about the *intention behind your question.* If you are truly asking a question to learn or understand, it will come across that way. Don't kid yourself: People *can* discern the difference between a true question vs. a challenge *shrouded* in a question.

Note: Using the word "you" in a question can be off-putting unless you are genuinely interested in the other person's opinion. In fact, one of the best questions you can ask in business, according to John C. Maxwell, is "What do *you* think?"

However, including the word "you" in a question when something bad happened or there's a problem simmering will likely come across as accusatory. For example, "Did you know about this?"

Take a look at the examples below of questions that fall into two categories: Better to avoid and best to leverage for an enriching conversation.

Better-to-Avoid Questions often include the words "Who," "Why," and "When." These nonproductive questions can feel like a fact-finding mission and tend to cause a defensive reflex:

- Are you responsible for this?
- Who said that?
- Why aren't you finished with the project?
- Why didn't you send an email?
- When were you going to share this information?

Best-to-Leverage Questions often include the words "What" and "How." These enriching questions are more indicative of a person *listening to understand*, and tend to invite a more open response:

- How did things go?
- What do you think happened?
- How did things get delayed?
- What else should I know about this situation?
- How can we do better next time?
- How is everyone feeling about this idea/solution?
- What do you need from me?
- How can I help?

P.S. Don't place blame. In business, things go wrong. That's to be expected. It's all about how you handle these moments. So, if you are asked the question, "What happened," or, "How did things get off track," your goal should be to give an honest assessment of the situation...with a solution. Dwelling on what went wrong or who-did-what doesn't help move things forward. So while it's perfectly acceptable to say in response: "There are things that could have gone more smoothly," or, "There are issues that need to be resolved," please don't be tempted to blame others. Blame statements are often subtle. Subtle or not, blame isn't a quality of a true leader. Here are a couple of veiled blame statements that I've heard:

- "I shouldn't have assumed that she would do her job."
- "Next time, I won't take others' words for granted."

All I can say is: Not cool, because if it has to do with your area of responsibility or someone on your team—I hold you responsible as the leader.

DISAGREEING WITH SOMEONE

There are times at The Table when you will find that you disagree with someone else's POV or that you want to offer a different perspective. There are effective ways to do this. Just as there are "openers" that work to establish receptivity in conversation, there are also *shut-down statements*—which kill conversation and can erode relationships. After a few awkward faux pas and blunders of my own, I have worked out a method that helps move conversations forward:

STEP #1: Bite your tongue—don't respond with a conversation shut-down statement
STEP #2: Seek common ground
STEP #3: Affirm then transition

STEP #1: Bite your tongue—don't respond with a shut-down statement

Remember the human factor? Even in the workplace, emotions and feelings come into play. So when you dialogue with someone and you disagree with what they are saying—take a deep breath, bite your tongue—do whatever it takes to **stop yourself** from firing off a shut-down statement such as:

- "I disagree..."
- "That's not how it happened..."
- "No..."

- "Yes, but..."
- And please don't silently shake your head *no* while they are speaking. It's undermining and it's a trigger for heated disagreements.

STEP #2: Seek common ground

When you realize that you disagree with what someone is saying, listen hard and calmly take a moment to figure out (in your head) what you can agree on—this is the common ground that you will want to share with the other person. It's the absolute best place to pivot from. By finding this common ground, you are affirming and validating someone else's POV and acknowledging their feelings. You bring down their defenses, defuse lingering tension, and lay some track to increase their receptivity to your idea. Affirmation only takes a moment. It enhances other people's hearing and it opens the doors to mutually beneficial situations...and it can easily be done in under 10 words.

Here's a few to try out:

- "I can understand how you would have that perspective."
- "We're essentially on the same page."
- "I agree with a lot of what you just said."

STEP #3: Affirm then transition

Now that their defenses have been lowered and tension is defused, it's time to give your differing opinion. You have moved them into a state of mind that is better primed to listen to what you have to say vs. in a state of mind that's fired up to defend their position.

Try out these affirm-then-transition statements:

- "We're basically on the same page when it comes to abc... where our views diverge is regarding xyz."

- "I agree with a lot of what you just said about abc...I'm not sure that you're aware of xyz."

LISTENING WITH YOUR EARS...AND WITH YOUR EYES

One of the most crucial and powerful skills in the business world is listening. When you *really* listen to what people are saying—especially to what they repeat and to what their body and facial language is communicating—you will be in the league of career women that operate on a much higher level of human truth.

Oftentimes, your colleagues are focusing on what they are going to say next instead of listening. As such, they are missing so many things that are going on right under their noses. They are missing out on the nuances that make all the difference in business relationships and negotiating. So, by listening—setting your focus to an outward vs. an inward perspective—you will be way ahead of the game.

What I'm asking you to do in these settings is to **actively listen**, like a detective trying to get a confession. Ask yourself what words or phrases they might be *repeating*. Yes, you should do a mental tally of how many times a senior leader, or a client, repeats something, because what people repeat are the things that matter to them—the things that are keeping them awake at night. Imagine how your "stock" will increase if you take note of these repeats and then surprise them with a solution—especially when they didn't ask for one.

The other thing you must listen for is the emotion that's *behind* their words. This emotion is best communicated by facial expressions and body language. In work settings, people tend to be polite and very selective with their words, but remember that the body doesn't lie. Ask yourself: *What are their body lan-*

guage and facial expressions REALLY telling me? It is estimated that only 7% of any message is communicated through words—the other 93% is nonverbal communication through body language and vocal elements.

Anthropologist Ray Birdwhistell estimated that the average person actually speaks words for a total of only 10 minutes a day and that the average sentence takes only about 2.5 seconds. (My husband would tell you that these averages don't apply to me.) Birdwhistell also estimated that we can make and recognize around 250,000 facial expressions.

What does all of this mean? Carefully observe people's **unspoken language.** This will arm you with a deeper perspective of what's truly going on. Albert Mehrabian's *Silent Messages* is the gold standard for interpreting nonverbal meaning.

There is one other thing you should do, especially if you're responsible for leading a team, and that's to *read the room.* There are three things to be mindful of, especially when you're the leader in this situation:

- Is there an elephant in the room?
- Is someone sending distress signals?
- Is everyone participating in the conversation?

Is there an elephant in the room?

This refers to an obvious problem, issue, or difficult situation that no one wants to confront but that everyone is aware of and trying to ignore.

As the leader at The Table, you should be conscious of and ready to surface and address any rumors, touchy subjects, and company "news" head-on. Don't ignore these undercurrents, hoping they will fade away. They do not take care of themselves and they are usually major distractors.

Is someone sending distress signals?

This refers to any nonverbal indication that something's up. Distress signals include a lowered head, fidgeting in the seat, and a deep sigh or a series of sighs–the little sounds people make when they're not happy about something.

As a leader, you should want your team to feel limitless and unstoppable. A simple "How're you feeling about x" is all it takes to signal that you recognize their distress, even if they aren't aware of the messages they've been sending. This will facilitate working toward a solution without any delays or lost time.

Is everyone participating in the conversation?

This refers to when a person who is typically engaged in conversations at The Table is holding back and not giving her opinion. This too signals that something could be afoot. Check in with this person to get a read on if something's up.

As leaders, if we ignore the elephant in the room, distress signals, or the typically engaged team member holding back—things will fester and people will stew. This can be very disruptive to the team dynamic and overall productivity. When you make it common practice to address issues, people can be heard and move on—and you can then expect to be better able to focus your team on the matters at hand.

Tackling these three situations only takes a moment. When you're the leader at The Table, this simple practice allows people to feel, and to be heard.

PROVIDING A BRIEFING

One of the other common conversations at The Table is a verbal executive summary—a briefing of a work-related situation that allows for senior management to become *rapidly* acquainted with the most important highlights of a large volume of information. Here's how it typically goes: A senior leader or your client asks you for an update on a particular situation, and you only have a couple of minutes to give them a rundown that succinctly provides key information: The need-to-knows. They want to know so they will be in-the-know—in case their managers ask them. Providing a good briefing is a skill that can help you to stand out among your peers.

To my ear, an impressive briefing has three components:

- An honest, balanced assessment
- Accountability
- A solution

I'm not a fan of the **"keep the boss happy" briefing:**

Lois: "How did this morning's digital presentation for Client X go?"

Response: "Oh, it went well. The clients were a little distracted, but we got through everything and they seemed to like the work."

Assessment: The person who tries to sell me on everything being *rosy*—whether to please me, or because they failed to read the room—sets up a false sense of security. If something *does* end up going wrong, we can get blindsided. We're not prepared to help them, the company, or the client. Course-correction is much more difficult when the only information I have is misleadingly positive.

I need to be able to trust the judgment of my team leaders, so if someone is telling me *it's all good* or *it's smooth sailing* when this isn't the case, it's a hell of a lot harder to get us back on track. And I'm going to have a difficult time trusting you the next time you suggest or say *no worries.*

If I had to choose, over the false-positive briefing I'd always opt for the **doom-and-gloom briefing** because at least it puts me on the alert:

Lois: "How did the digital presentation for Client X go?"

Response: "Oh, it was rough. The clients were totally distracted—focused on their phones and, when they weren't buried in their screens, they were in and out of the room. We barely got through everything. On top of that, their polite reaction to the presentation made it clear they considered it lackluster."

Assessment: At least with this briefing, we're on the alert. The problem with this doom-and-gloom briefing is that it's *missing a solution*...the path forward to a resolution with this client.

What I'm really looking for is what I call a **balanced briefing.** I'm reminded of someone who did this masterfully. She's a driving force who sparkles with intelligence, passion, and confidence. She always gave me the honest low-down. No sugarcoating. And she *always* brought a solution.

Lois: "How did the digital presentation for Client X go?"

Response: "When we arrived, they were running late, so they seemed somewhat distracted. This isn't typical for them, so we asked if everything was okay. We learned that there was a big restructuring happening this week. We got through the presentation, but their reaction suggested that we'd missed the mark. I was the one who recommended we go in this direction, so that's on me. We've put a follow-up teleconference on for early next week when things on their end have settled back down over there—and we've had the chance to revise our materials."

Assessment: A true awareness of the presentation—the good, the bad, the uncertain—means we're appropriately alerted. Balanced information allows us to pivot with *eyes wide open* onto a path forward.

A WINNING BRIEFING =

TRUTH + OWNERSHIP + SOLUTION

And when I observe a team member taking accountability? Well, that is a beautiful thing. By bringing the truth and offering me a solution, I know that you have a plan—which instills confidence in me. Smart, well-reasoned solutions and clear-headed awareness means that you are thinking like an owner, which makes you shine in my eyes. And those who shine are noticed.

So ask yourself—what kind of briefings do you give at The Table. Rosy? Doom-and-gloom? Balanced?

As we close out this chapter–the seven essential components of earning your seat at The Table–I want to pull all of this information together for you with one main takeaway: The effort and energy that you put into your career will have a direct impact on the outcome. Your career advancement–to be viewed as a leader and respected–hinges on *you*.

Emmy and Grammy award winner, Steve Martin, puts it this way:

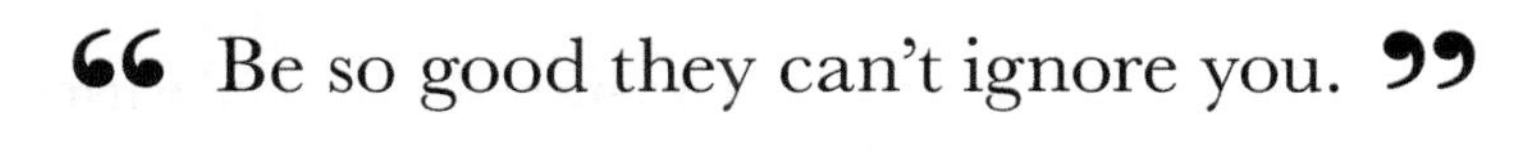
Be so good they can't ignore you.

AT-THE-TABLE VOLTA MOMENTS

As you think about your seat at The Table, use the lines below to reflect whether you have experienced any illuminations related to:

- Your preparation
- Your daily power sessions
- Your consideration of the big picture
- Your active listening skills
- Your dialoguing at The Table
- Your briefings at The Table

ACTIONS

Declare below what you will start doing right away to earn and secure your seat at The Table:

____

____

____

____

____

VOLTA TRADE SECRET

#3

HOW TO HAVE COURAGEOUS CONVERSATIONS

A person's level of success *directly* correlates with their ability to have courageous conversations.

At the age of 91, my stepdad, while eating lunch, got a large piece of chicken lodged in his airway. The paramedics came and worked on him to clear the obstruction but he had been without oxygen for more than a couple of minutes. As soon as Marc and I got to my mom's house, the three of us headed straight to the emergency room. We sat for a while in the waiting area. I didn't have a good feeling at all.

A patient advocate showed up and brought us to a private room. We weren't there long before two young physicians joined us—

one was the attending physician of the ER and the other was the ICU resident. I was sitting right next to the attending physician—it was she who kicked off the conversation. The alarm bells were going off in my head. She was there to deliver bad news. She couldn't have been more than 30. Her presence was warm and confident. I took note of the slight tremor in her right hand.

Like a pro, she handled one of the most difficult conversations that *anyone* ever has to have. As I listened to her, it became evident that she wasn't winging it—she was using a specific approach, a well-practiced formula. First, she asked my mother if she realized what had happened. Her strategy was to get *my mother* to be the one to say out loud how severe the situation was. This paved the way for her to deliver the grave news about my stepdad's medical condition. She painted a very realistic picture, but she also offered a sliver of hope–it was important to her how she left us feeling. She was masterful, and the formula she employed was *exactly* what we needed as a family in this situation.

Dad passed away the next morning—comfortable and without any pain. The physician, whom I will always remember, helped to make a very difficult situation more bearable. With her courage, her kindness, and a perfected *conversation method,* she helped us *receive* what we needed to hear during this very difficult situation.

In the workplace, there are also several difficult but necessary conversations that go a lot smoother when the right method is employed. I refer to these as Courageous Conversations, and I have found these five to be the most common categories:

- Clearing the air with a boss, colleague, client, or employee
- Asking for a raise or a promotion

- Winning the support of others
- Delivering bad news
- Saying no

These are often internalized as dreaded conversations. Many times when we have to have one of these conversations we procrastinate, we avoid, we stall. There's usually some anxiety and often we lose sleep over it. But if your goal is to move ahead in your career, you *must learn* to face these tough conversations head-on. When I say to face them head-on, I don't expect you to approach them like a bull in a china shop. I just don't want you to avoid them, hoping they'll go away—because they won't.

Mastering Courageous Conversations is very doable—it just requires some prep time and some practice. There's no need to avoid them, and there's no need to fumble your way through them. In this chapter, I will share proven formulas—yes, there are proven formulas—that will make these conversations a hell of a lot easier and much more productive for you.

Assess your current level of confidence with the Courageous-Conversations-Meter

Take a look at the self-assessment scale that follows, and circle where you are in the land of facing tough conversations head-on. (Low score? No worries—you will become a pro with some practice!)

1	2	3	4	5	6	7	8	9	10

Avoidance Getting better Holding my own I'm a pro

CLEARING THE AIR

Nobody really likes conflict. We all know how it feels and how uncomfortable it can be. A meeting that doesn't go well, harsh words that were said, or a misunderstanding that occurs. You're left struggling to get through the day with a low-grade pit in your stomach. It might even trigger what I refer to as a *rumination attack*. This is when you turn over and over in your mind something that troubles you, without moving toward a solution. The next morning is no better—you're anxious and worried and wondering how long it will take for this uncomfortable, unsettling situation to be resolved.

In my experience, it's better to address the issue as soon as possible because the other person is probably feeling the same way but doesn't know how to resolve it either. Generally, these things don't just *go away* on their own.

The good news is that there's a proven method for having these conversations that works really well. The book *Crucial Conversations* delves deeply into this subject. This method involves specific steps that are simple to follow—and you can count on this method to yield a resolution, with a path forward.

Before you make your move, collect your thoughts and be sure that you have a grasp on your objective, then follow these 7 fast-moving steps that take a total of 5–15 minutes.

STEP #1. The very first thing you have to do is **throw the idea right out the window that "I'm right and you're wrong."** This mindset is a huge barrier toward resolution. This kind of black-and-white thinking—that someone is wrong and someone is right—is what *divides* us. It's the exact *opposite* mindset that's needed for conflict resolution. The right mindset for these situations is one that resides in the gray zone. The gray zone is where we accept our own flaws and the flaws of our fellow humans. This is the place where the healing can begin.

STEP #2. Set aside time to talk. Ask them when it would be a good time to catch up to talk things through. Don't just show up at their doorstep and expect things to go well...it probably won't, because people need time to get mentally prepared to talk.

STEP #3. Open with an honest statement—without assigning any blame. When the time for the conversation arrives, open with an honest statement such as, *I feel bad about how things went yesterday* and *I was hoping we could talk things through.*

STEP #4. Ask how they feel about things and then listen with both ears. Just by listening, you are well on your way to a solution. Allow the other person the time and judgment-free space to explain how the experience made them feel. Go ahead and take notes. In my experience, taking notes makes people feel heard and it signals that what they're sharing is very important to you.

- ***Your #1 objective is to get the other person to express their feelings.*** If they don't share their feelings in some way, they will continue to harbor hurt and won't be able to truly move forward.
- ***There is a technique you can rely on to help the other person get closer to their feelings.*** This technique is a method of questioning that involves deliberately including a portion of what the other person just said to you—embedded in a more targeted question. I've heard this referred to as both "Sherlocking" and "mirroring." This allows the other person to go deeper into their psyche. For example, if they say: "And then you interrupted me and changed subjects." You say: "You are upset because I interrupted you..." This will likely prompt them to share a deeper lev-

el of explanation: "Yes, you interrupted me just as I was going to share why changing the direction of the project could impact the timeline..."

STEP #5. Use a *validating statement* to acknowledge what they just shared *before* you begin to share your perspective on the matter. This is a crucial step—to acknowledge their feelings out loud, because it allows you the opportunity to move toward your perspective while conveying grace and dignity for the other person. Here are some options that I like a lot:

- "I see where you're coming from"
- "I hear you, and I get why you felt that way"
- "That must have been tough"
- "I understand your perspective much better now"

STEP #6. Now it's your turn. Once you've verbally acknowledged the other person's feelings, it's time to share your perspective on the experience—again without assigning blame. Remember: You must throw the notion of "I'm right and you're wrong" out of the window. It's useless, unproductive, and childish.

STEP #7. Move the conversation to the path forward together. You are now ready to move *together* toward a solution. Just like people don't like conflict, they also desire a resolution—so more than likely they will want to move forward with you. One way to phrase this:

- "I'm so glad we talked about this. Can we talk about how we can move forward from here?"

ASKING FOR A RAISE OR A PROMOTION

As you can imagine, silently hoping that someone will notice you and offer you a raise or a promotion isn't an effective strategy. When it comes to asking for a raise or a promotion, you will have a much better outcome if you follow a process of **three check-in conversations.** This particular Courageous Conversation is not going to be a "one-and-done." Asking for more money or responsibility is a phased process that you should expect to take at least 3–6 months from the starting point.

Check-in #1: Setting the stage

Start by requesting a time to set aside for a performance check-in—don't catch someone when they're on the run. They will want to be prepared for this kind of conversation. During your time together, you do want to make it clear that you are interested in getting to the next level and that you would really appreciate their counsel and perspective on helping you with a plan forward. In this meeting, touch on three things:

- Define your current level's roles and responsibilities and how you believe you are meeting or exceeding them.
- Request a description of the responsibilities for the next level. Ask your manager to compare and contrast the new more senior role to your current role.
- Affirm your intention to work toward the new role—ask what areas you should concentrate on to get to that higher level.

Check-in #2: Getting feedback

Allow approximately three months to pass before you request this follow-up. The purpose of this time together is for you to get feedback:

- Start by regrounding, by giving an overview, of what was covered during your last check-in.
- Outline your progress since you last met. Ask for their feedback and their observations.

- Ask them what they recommend you should be striving to improve to get you to your goal.

Check-in #3: Performance review time

By now, you have had two check-ins and there should be no surprises. Here's how you want to shape your part in this conversation:

- Briefly restate your goals and provide, in clear and concise terms, your achievements.
- Declare yourself "ready."
- Genuinely seek their additional perspective.
- If the answer is "You're not ready," get their feedback and ask to regroup at a later date. If they welcome the idea, with specific guidance, I would say that's promising.
- Ask about their 6–12 month vision for you on their team and/or with the company. This will be very telling.
- If specifics aren't offered regarding a 6-month vision for you, and you're getting clear signals that there's no path forward, it might be time to reconsider if the current situation holds promise for your career aspirations. It could also be an indicator that this is not the career that aligns with your strengths.

WINNING THE SUPPORT OF OTHERS

There are going to be times in your career when you need to persuade—to win the support of others to collaborate with you. It might have to do with an idea, with a vision, or even simply for them to get involved in something that requires a change from the familiar.

You will need to describe what you are envisioning, with clarity, but it's equally important to also **get them to visualize themselves** in the picture you paint. That's the WIIFM factor—the "What's In It For Me?" Sharing the vision is good, but sharing a vision with how *they* will personally benefit is much more compelling.

YOUR VISION + WIIFM = PERSUASION POWER

This method is especially powerful when you are charged with initiating something challenging that requires others to collaborate with you—especially when they don't report to you. Every time you are preparing to have this type of Courageous Conversation, you need to ask yourself: *What's in it for them?* Be sure to weave these insights into the story that you lay out for them.

Here's a personal example of how I put the persuasive power of WIIFM to work. In the agency world, your success is tightly linked to your team's success. This is because, at an agency, you can have great strategic ideas—but if you can't bring these ideas to life via the creative product in a way that moves your clients (and their customers), you got nothin'. As such, the Account Teams and the Creative Teams have a codependency for achieving success. At work, this codependency is more common than you might think. This dynamic calls for finding a WIIFM for the other team members.

There was this occasion where one of our biggest clients was figuring out how to get pediatricians to see an established brand in a new light, so that they would expand its use for more of their patients. This would require additional research time, copy time, and design time—and the client needed it right away. (Of course they did.)

How do you convince your team to get excited about a rush project when they're already super busy? (Did I mention that none of these folks reported to me?) I took some time to figure out how my goals aligned with *their goals* and then I helped them to envision how our shared success would play out. I picture-painted the day of the client presentation–how they would shine as they delivered their creative solution to the client's dilemma. This helped them *feel* how significant the accomplishment would be for *themselves*.

When that day came, they were heroes. Their stock went up, the agency's stock went up, and the client's stock went up. Get the people you work with to envision how *they will benefit* and you will be successful, together. In the words of bestselling author Zig Ziglar:

> “You can have everything in life *you* want, if you will just help other people get what *they* want.”

DELIVERING BAD NEWS

The fact is that when you get to a certain level in the business world, you will be responsible for delivering bad news. It's never easy—and it likely never will get any easier. This is a Courageous Conversation that no one wants to have, but delivering bad news must be done.

Odds are many of those who have gathered to hear this news already have a sense that the news you're going to tell them isn't good. Whether a team member has been let go, the company has been acquired, or there has been a layoff—it is important to be straightforward with those who are looking to you in this time of turmoil.

As with the other Courageous Conversations, there's an effective formula for delivering bad news.

- Open with what you are there to share: "We had to let Barry go" or "The company has been bought out" or "We've had to lay off several people."
- Move swiftly to your deeply felt thoughts regarding how difficult the decision was—*personalize* the news with your human struggle with this decision.
- Then it's time to share:
    - How it is in the best interest of them/the health of the business, which directly impacts them and their families
    - Why this had to happen
- Move to a close with a Q&A session, or say that your door is always open if anyone wants to speak with you.

SAYING NO

It can be hard to say no. The higher you ascend in the business world, the more you'll find yourself having to say it. We can be uncomfortable with saying no—it can feel harsh and it can bring feelings of guilt. So you have probably heard yes come out of your mouth when your brain is saying a definitive no. And here's the problem with that—by saying yes to something when you should actually be saying no, the likelihood is that you'll end up disappointing them anyway by not following through, not showing up, or failing to deliver.

After a string of these letdowns, people will stop trusting you. Your word becomes questionable. Resentment and mistrust build—all because you were uncomfortable with letting your no mean no and your yes mean yes. Bottom line: Stop trying to make everyone happy by saying yes all of the time when you don't mean it. You'll end up with the very *opposite* effect of what you were trying to achieve in the first place—they're not going to be happy, and neither are you.

In the workplace, it's frequently about yes and no—so it's important that you get comfortable with saying no when you mean no. Here's what I recommend:

- First, make sure that you have the information you need to decide on your answer. Ask enough questions to determine the true scope of the offer or request.
- With this information, ask yourself, *Can I do this? Do I want to do this?* Allow yourself to sleep on it when someone makes a big request. This way, you give yourself some processing time to give an honest yes or no.
- If the answer is no, then you owe them that honest answer.
- Be brief. Don't get lost in excuses. It's appropriate to say "I can't" or "I'm not able to." Be clear, because if you're too vague, they might think you actually agreed to their request.
- Use language that's clear but not brash. For example:
  - "I would like to help, but..."
  - "I can't commit now—it's a hectic time"
- Offer an alternative, but *only* if it's genuine. For example, if you are swamped, tell the person making the request that you'd like to help but that you will only be freed up after you meet your current deadline.

Courageous Conversations are career-defining and they do require courage. Now that you have learned these secret formulas, you are much better equipped to succeed. With some practice, things will become even easier. People will take notice of how smoothly you are handling these conversations. Don't be surprised when they "model" your methods.

You can expect your skill with facing and handling Courageous Conversations to correlate directly with your promotability and what you can command in salary. There's another important benefit to all of this: People will *feel good* about their interactions with you. In the words of poet and singer, Maya Angelou:

> "I've learned that people will forget what you said, people will forget what you did, but people will never forget how you made them feel."

COURAGEOUS CONVERSATIONS VOLTA MOMENTS

So, as you think about your ability to have Courageous Conversations, use the lines below to write whether you have had any illuminations regarding:

- Clearing the air
- Asking for a raise or promotion
- Winning the support of others
- Delivering bad news
- Saying no

____

____

ACTIONS

Declare below what you will start doing right away to enhance your comfort and confidence with Courageous Conversations:

____

____

____

____

____

VOLTA TRADE SECRET

#4

HOW TO UNLEARN AND LEAD

Leadership is a paradox.
It seems to be *this* but it's actually *that*.

When I set out to write *Career VOLTA*, I purposely decided *not* to write a book about leadership. That book has been written, many times, by some pretty impressive thought-leaders. However, since this is a book for career women, I'd be remiss to not at least touch on the topic of leadership. So, here goes. Lois on leadership...

If you think of leadership as a *verb*, instead of a noun, it brings clarity to a potentially elusive concept. In its most distilled state, leadership is about what you do. It's about action. It's about influencing and motivating a group of people to take action toward achieving a common goal. Leaders inspire people through a shared vision. They create an environment where people feel valued and inspired. What you do and say impacts how people feel. When they feel inspired and valued, they will remember and refer to you long after your time together. As said by well-known broadcast industry executive, Donald McGannon:

> "Leadership is an action, not a position."

Assess your skills with the Leadership-Meter

Take a look at the self-assessment scale that follows, and circle your current level of leadership skills. (Don't worry—leadership is not usually something you're born with. It takes practice!)

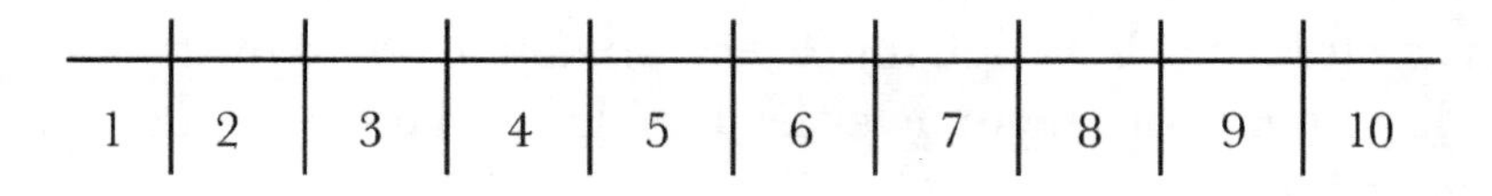

Starting out   Getting better   Holding my own   Sought-after leader

MY FIRST LEADERSHIP POSITION

Take a look at the list below. This list of qualities stood out for me as I moved into my first leadership position. I was on my way. I was an up-and-comer.

UP-AND-COMER
Gets it done
Pushes onward
A strong force
Expert speaker
Has the answers
Comfortable in the spotlight
Understands complex concepts
Strives to please the team
Gets noticed
Takes pride
Tough negotiator
Wins
MOTTO:
"I will make this happen"

THE PARADOX

While this seems like a worthy list of leadership traits to strive for, the truth is that these are not the traits that we like having in our leaders. That's why I refer to leadership as a paradox. A paradox is defined as a "seemingly absurd proposition that when investigated or explained actually proves to be well-informed and true."

In the case of leadership, this list, while it does reflect admirable human traits, reflects traits that are largely and surprisingly the **opposite** of what is associated with a *beloved* leader—a leader who people clamor to work for.

In fact, most of us have worked for a "leader" with the traits on this list. We know how we feel when we work for one of these characters: We feel awful, because we know in our bones that they care more about their success than they care about ours.

AT THE HEART OF THIS PARADOX

Yes, it's true that during the early years of our career, we have to prove ourselves—it's the time to push hard, to learn everything we can about our field, to gain mastery, and to get noticed for it.

I can remember those years like they were yesterday. I could feel hot liquid coursing through my veins. It was pure, unabashed ambition. I was hungry. I was acutely focused on proving myself, moving up the ladder, and getting promoted. This was my #1 priority. I didn't see the others around me—they were on the periphery of my intense self-focus.

Because of my achievements, I was given a team of five to report to me at the age of 25. So what did I do? I pretty much continued to do many of the same things—push, achieve, work hard, and get noticed. I actually worked even harder. I took on a lot of my team's workload. This way, it would be done on time and it would be done right. I gave all the presentations. I mapped out the plans. I ran all the meetings. I made all the decisions. Dear God, they must have hated me.

THE DAY OF RECKONING

My job is to tell you the truth. And here it is. In order to truly succeed in your career, you must *continually strive* to become a good leader of people. It's not a choice, it's a requirement. You too will have to have that day of reckoning, if you haven't already had it. You will need to do something, very specific, that all leaders-in-the-making have to do: Transform from a self-driven high achiever to a beloved leader that people will follow to the ends of the earth. You will have to cross over this very real line in the sand. The side you start on is the *me*-side. The side you must cross over to is the *them*-side.

When you first cross over, it's going to feel strange. It feels like the opposite of common sense. Hence the paradox that I referred to. When you have truly crossed over the line into leadership mode, you accept that it's no longer about your needs. It's about the needs of your *team*. It's no longer about your conquests. It's about their conquests. You move out of the spotlight. They move in. You drop back. They move forward. I trust you're getting the picture.

Someone who is very dear to me asked if this phrase should be worded as the *us*-side instead of the *them*-side. Because I have such deep respect for her opinions, I pondered making this edit. I decided to sleep on it. The next morning, while making my coffee (Sumatra with lots of half & half), I decided to keep it as *them*-side and not *us*. Here's why. Yes, it's true that it's a matter of the leader plus her team. However, since it's *crucial* that a leader puts their people first and not themselves, I stuck with the original phrase of *them*-side.

Think about a leader that you love or loved working with. What is it about them that you admire? What makes you feel good when you think about being on their team? Take a look at both sides of the following chart. Chances are the leaders you admire demonstrate a lot of the traits on the right-hand column vs. the traits on the left.

THE PARADOX OF LEADERSHIP

UP-AND-COMER	BELOVED LEADER
Gets it done	Delegates and empowers
Pushes onward	Persuades with a vision
A strong force	A calming force
Expert speaker	Expert listener
Has the answers	Has great questions
Comfortable in the spotlight	Puts the spotlight on the team
Understands complex concepts	Simplifies complex concepts
Strives to please the team	Willing to be unpopular
Gets noticed	Gets the team noticed
Takes pride	Has humility
Tough negotiator	Lets people save face
Wins	Wins minds and hearts
MOTTO:	**MOTTO:**
"I will make this happen"	"We will make this happen"

The leadership qualities in the right-hand column are timeless. As we move into leadership positions, we have to *very* mindfully absorb these into the fabric of who we are—because these qualities are, practically speaking, the opposite of what got us promoted. That's what makes it a paradox.

ARE LEADERS BORN OR MADE?

I'm often asked: Is leadership something people are born with? I am 100% resolute in my answer: Leadership is a learned set of skills that *can be acquired*. But know this—at the heart of all these skills is the distinctive mindset of my team vs. me. It's that simple. And yet it's not that easy. Bottom line—leaders are self-made. So why not make the decision to be a sought-after leader?

MY ONGOING LEADERSHIP JOURNEY

Each day I *strive* to be what I refer to as a "magnanimous leader." This is the kind of leader who has three standout qualities: vision, purpose driven, and lionhearted.

A person with *vision* looks forward, into the future, to see what's down the road, and then prepares for that future. A visionary leader sees the potential of the people entrusted to their care. This leader generously shares with their people the greatness they see in them—privately and *publicly*. They are encouragers. And instead of avoiding tough conversations, they discuss needed performance improvements—with kindness and, always, behind closed doors.

To be *purpose driven* means to move forward every day with a plan, with positivity and with zest. Since we only have so much energy to give to each day, our goal should be to focus our energy toward achieving this purpose, and to minimize distractions.

Lionhearted is a description that someone very dear to me asked me to explain. For me, it means to have a really big heart for people—your team, your clients, your peers, and your leaders. With certain people that you work with, you will have to dig deep to find something to love about them. This big heart brings many lasting relationships and it lets you forgive. Sometimes a big heart can be a problem because, with it, you see the *best* in people, so watch out for developing blind spots—it can happen. It's happened to me a couple of times. However, the relationships I've enjoyed over the years far outweigh the risk.

DISPELLING THE MYTH, ONCE AND FOR ALL

So when you take all of this into consideration—that true leadership challenges conventional wisdom and is, in fact, the opposite of what you might have thought it was—it's time to address the myth...

Myth: A strong female leader will always be thought of as a bitch.

I don't buy into that. Not for one second. Here's what I think. I've been referred to as "tough" many times but *never* a bitch. I believe this is because I've crossed over to the *them*-side and the people on my team know I have *their* best interest at heart, not my own. They feel that I want *them* to shine, not me. President John Quincy Adams described it this way:

> "If your actions inspire others to dream more, do more, and become more, you are a leader."

We've all encountered unsavory leaders in our lives, women and men alike. The problem is that they haven't crossed over from the *me*-side to the *them*-side. For whatever reason, perhaps low self-esteem or a lack of self-awareness, they are stuck on the *me*-side of that line in the sand.

Don't be one of "those" leaders. Make that deliberate choice to step over to the *them*-side and savor the joy and satisfaction of helping people find their greatness. Trust me, they will always remember you and you will become the benchmark of their future bosses.

Ryan Gromfin, a.k.a. The Restaurant Boss, captures the leadership concept perfectly:

> “ Be the kind of leader that *you* would follow. ”

LEADERSHIP PARADOX VOLTA MOMENTS

So, as you think about the kind of leader you are, write on the lines below if you have experienced any illuminations regarding:

- The paradox of being a leader
- If you're on the *me*-side or the *them*-side
- The B-word myth

____

____

____

ACTIONS

Declare below what you will start doing right away to ensure that you live on the *them*-side of the leadership line:

____

____

____

____

____

VOLTA TRADE SECRET

#5

HOW TO STRENGTHEN YOUR MOXIE MUSCLE

Holding things in your business life at a healthy distance takes *moxie*.

For many years, I let things that happened at work get to me. My recovery time was way too long and I didn't have very effective coping techniques. Too many times I would come home at the end of the day bursting at the seams with an incident that caused hurt and anger. I would go on and on with who said what and who did what. Poor Marc. I think that's when he learned the art of repeating the word "right" while he (pretended) to listen to one of my recaps of a bad day.

I didn't want to feel that way, I wanted relief from these symptoms. As with most things in life, no one was going to do it for me. I was the one who had to figure out how to work through, better yet *prevent*, these joy-robbing situations.

What I needed was moxie. Think of your favorite female character on TV, in a book, in a movie. Who has the attitude, the strength, and the bold spirit that you admire most? Is it someone like Olivia Pope from *Scandal*, or C.J. Cregg from *The West Wing*, or Katniss Everdeen from *The Hunger Games*?

They all have well-honed Moxie Muscle.

Moxie Muscle is the 5th Trade Secret that will give you a distinct advantage in the workplace. This Trade Secret brings a way of thinking with *active techniques* that you can use to hold things in your business life objectively—at a distance—with a healthy perspective. It's important to maintain a wholesome relationship with your work so that you can live with gusto. For many of us, this will require us to retrain our brains on some fronts.

MENTAL TOUGHNESS + GRIT + RESILIENCE = MOXIE

A career woman with moxie is able to shake things off. She's a determined person who doesn't give up easily. And she's learned to create a healthy distance between herself and the politics, egos, posturing, and power struggles that are all around her in the work environment. By using her Moxie Muscle, she proactively prevents this source of negativity from seeping into her spirit. She puts her mindset to work *for* her and her inner dialogue, too. She's a curious learner; these are some of the things she says to herself:

- *I've got this!*
- *What's the worst that can happen?*
- *I fail fast. I learn. I move on from my setbacks.*

Having the right attitude is vital because your attitude is a rare example of something that's actually 100% within your direct control.

Assess the strength of your Moxie Muscle

Take a look at the self-assessment scale that follows, and circle the current status of your Moxie Muscle. (If your Moxie Muscle is a bit flabby, don't stress—we'll get it toned and in shape in no time!)

1	2	3	4	5	6	7	8	9	10

Undeveloped I can feel it growing! I can see it! I'm fully pumped!

If you don't feel like you have enough, or any, Moxie Muscle, you're not alone in this. It doesn't usually come naturally—it takes mindfulness, learning specific techniques, and then practicing them. Personally, I want the biggest dose of moxie that's possible for any human being to have because the more Moxie Muscle you have, the more fun and joy you will have in your life!

Growing and developing your Moxie Muscle should be a top priority for yourself because, at the end of the day, per Michael Corleone from *The Godfather*, "It's not personal. It's business."

We will focus on the following 5 Moxie Muscle fortifiers:

- The VOLTA To-Do List
- Thick skin
- Gut instinct
- Financial freedom
- Reframing vs. rehashing

THE VOLTA TO-DO LIST

The VOLTA To-Do List is one of those *wow things* that will bring a great ROI (return on investment). It's really easy and it will bring *instant positive change to your life.* Many career women already follow a to-do list, but the kind of list that I'm recommending has two specific sections that will make a big impact on your progress.

Let's face it—life happens. Everyone is super busy these days, even my retired parents. My point is this: You can cram every day with lots of things to do, but here's the question to ask yourself: *"Is what I'm doing every day bringing me closer to my vision for myself...closer to my dream?"*

Because of this realization I had about 10 years ago—that we can be really busy but not progressing—I amped up my to-do list to make sure that I move the ball forward, every week, toward my life goals and dreams.

The VOLTA To-Do List will have a direct impact on the direction of your life because it brings you this control and a much-needed focus on your specific priorities. It puts you in the driver's seat of your life by prioritizing your days and weeks to include action steps that will propel you forward toward your life's mission and purpose. I believe you will find this to be empowering.

Here's how it works. You are going to use one surface—a page from a dedicated notebook or a Word document—that's divided into two sections. They are:

SECTION #1: My Day

In this section, you list out what you have to get done today. Many of us already keep this kind of list. Examples of this are: depositing a check, creating project timelines, pulling together a status meeting, calling your client.

Here's what's new: Add *a must do something that scares me* every day. This advice comes directly from Eleanor Roosevelt. It could include things like introducing yourself to someone that you admire, speaking up at a meeting, eating kale :)

SECTION #2: My Dream

This new, critical section will be dedicated to moving your dream/vision for yourself forward so that when you look back in 6-12 months, you're able to see steady progress toward reaching your career goals. Examples of this are: updating your resume, attending a digital seminar, cultivating an important business relationship, creating a website.

Also use this new section to:

- Add something to look forward to each week. Examples of these "me-time" activities are: getting a massage, taking a day trip, watching that movie you've been wanting to see.
- Include things that you need *stop* doing. These are the things that are taking up your precious time, focus, and energy. They are diverting your attention *away* from achieving your new dream/vision for yourself. Examples of this are: lunching with people at work who bring you down, skipping workouts, spending too much time on social media.

I'll leave you with this thought-provoking little parable–my last pitch for making your VOLTA To-Do List a source of empowerment...

The first woman fills her thoughts each day with making her first $1M. The second woman focuses her thoughts on making 50 sales calls and how she plans to enjoy each of these conversations. Who is more likely to succeed? Answer: The second woman, because she is focusing her energies on what she can control. The first woman is focusing on what she can't control.

Make your VOLTA To-Do List a habit, something that you faithfully do for yourself. This will give you all the benefits that come with placing your focus on something that you can actually *control* on your road to success.

THICK SKIN

The workplace can be the most invigorating, adrenaline-producing place to be—where teamwork and the vast possibility of accomplishment is there for the taking. But the workplace can also be a harsh environment. There's a lot of comparison going on, jockeying for attention, competing for budget dollars—and the highs and lows that come with winning and losing. So you need to wear your thick skin to work to be better equipped to recover—to shake things off vs. letting negativity seep into your heart and soul. Bestselling author Deborah Shames, from one of my all-time favorite books, *Out Front*, is succinct on this topic:

> “Women need to develop thicker skins.”

I'm just going to say it. From where I sit, I have observed that women tend to have a hard time depersonalizing work-related matters, and we also tend to beat ourselves up for longer periods of time than necessary. Please know that I include myself in this group. Frankly, the women on my team are often the most highly valued—because they are very serious about success, they are unstoppable, and they have an intense work ethic. This is wonderful, as long as it doesn't come at a price—with consequences like losing sleep, not being able to hit the off-switch, depression, and exhaustion. We've all been there and it's not pretty, is it?

Here's what I recommend to keep things at a healthy distance and to *shake things off* more efficiently:

- **Find the kernel of truth in criticism that you receive.** When someone gives you feedback that makes you feel criticized, the best response is usually to say, "Thank you for your perspective." When you have time to take a step back from the situation—to digest what you heard—you will want to contemplate the *source* of this feedback and the *value* of this feedback. Oftentimes we can find *something* that brings value and holds truth in the feedback we receive. Extract it and keep what's beneficial to you–then let it go and move on.
- **View your failures as gifts.** It's no fun to encounter setbacks, to make mistakes, to fail. Yet it happens to every single one of us. Setbacks are inevitable. They are tough to experience but they shape us. Failure is not the enemy. Quite the opposite—failure is our best teacher. Admit your failures and mistakes. Extract all of the learnings, the *gifts*, and tuck them away for the future—I *guarantee* you that you'll have another opportunity to apply these learnings and it will feel really good.

- **Limit your *beat-yourself-up-sessions*.** Many of us replay our mistakes over and over again in our heads. We wish we had done or said things differently. This self-flagellation can go on for days–yet it's such an unproductive use of your time. I can't tell you how many times I've seen a woman on my team beat herself up for several days, even weeks, over a mistake that she made. To stop this self-torture, you are going to take 15 minutes, that's it, to figure out what you *learned* from this setback, write it down very objectively—and then turn over the page and force yourself onward.
- **Let go and laugh at yourself.** Have a big ol' belly laugh when you do or say something imperfect. Remember that you are human and people want you to be human, not a perfect robot. Please don't take yourself too seriously. It makes for a person who is inflexible, defensive, and boorish. I should know; I was one of those people.
- **Purposely look for the funny things in situations.** There's usually something that's humorous, even in the most intense business situations. If you take a moment to *appropriately* highlight one of them, it lightens the mood. The laughter that happens in the room often serves as a trigger for people's brains to click into a more creative, problem-solving mode.
- **Enjoy the benefits of forgiveness.** I did not invent this notion of the benefits of forgiveness. It's a highly discussed topic. On YouTube, I found 6.04 million results related to forgiveness. Every single one of us has been hurt by someone's actions or words. We've been cut deep. It churns us up, it makes us angry, it brings tears. And yet, we need to find forgiveness in our hearts because unforgiveness is toxic—it's poison for our souls. Many times, people don't even realize that they've hurt us. So please do *yourself* a really big favor, and forgive them. All of them. It will be

> very freeing, and it comes with other benefits. According to the world-renowned Mayo Clinic, forgiveness can lead to improved mental health, less anxiety, lower blood pressure, fewer symptoms of depression, a stronger immune system, improved heart health, and improved self-esteem.

I'm certain that I've unintentionally hurt people along the way—I hope they can find it in their heart to forgive me too.

Bottom line: You're tougher than you think. Set time limits for critical self-reflection; give yourself the gift of laughter; get really good at viewing your setbacks objectively. Extract all you can from your mistakes then deliberately *shake things off and move forward.*

GUT INSTINCT

The workplace is an *echo chamber* filled with opinions, recommendations, data, and bottom lines. It can be a struggle to navigate all of these opinions and recommendations. From experience I have learned to stop and ask myself what my gut instinct has to say about important situations.

It is now acknowledged that our gut functions as our "second brain." It's that inner sense in the pit of the stomach—when something just doesn't quite sit well. It can also be a *prompting* to step out of your comfort zone.

We've all had this experience. The concept of our gut being our second brain has become a highly studied area of research. It boils down to our vagus nerve, and how it intersects with our gut and our central nervous system. Based on your anatomy and physiology, your gut has been storing years of information and data for as long as you've been alive. As such, it's a great source of both promptings and warnings.

To prove this to yourself—jot down a couple of times you made a decision that aligned with *trusting your gut*. Wasn't the outcome usually positive?

____

____

In contrast, what happened those times that you didn't listen to your gut? Did you have any regrets?

____

____

I know first-hand how *not listening* to my gut instinct became a big regret...

I was fired from a job for non-business related purchases being placed on the master bill at a company-sponsored event. It was a very different time in the pharmaceutical industry—a climate of *anything goes*. During this time, putting everything on the master bill was common practice. But I had very bad timing because, as it turns out, the corporate auditing team was on a mission to make it stop—to make an example of the consequences of this practice. Since I was the most senior person at the event, I took the hit. For me, what resulted was a humiliating investigation and getting fired. What I did was wrong—my gut was *urging* me to listen—but I got sucked into the vortex of "everyone is doing it" and, more importantly, I paid the price for not listening to my gut. I don't want something like this to *ever happen to you*—that's why I'm sharing this painful memory.

There was a another time in my life, when thankfully, I listened to what my gut was saying despite what my brain was saying to me...

I was in my late thirties. I had crossed over from the client side of the Pharma industry to the agency side. This required me to commute by train from New Jersey to NYC every day. This commute was almost two hours each way. I was determined to use this time for reading and working. Well, that lasted about two months. Harry, the "train mayor," was on my train (the 8:02) every morning. He wanted to be my friend. The more I tried to ignore him, shoving my nose into a book, hoping he'd take the hint, the more he persisted. For the longest time, I wouldn't even tell him my name. So he nicknamed me T-bone.

As I said, my brain kept saying *no*. I didn't want to give up this me-time on the train to hang out with Harry. But after months of this avoidance game, I decided to give into my gut instinct, which was nudging me to see where this relationship would take me. Turns out, Harry is an accountant in private practice. As he got to know me and watched the way I worked, he became determined to get me to start my own business. He would say at least once a week: "You need to start your own business. You work harder than all of these schmucks and look how successful they are!" So after three years of his constant *campaigning*, I took his advice, and the rest is history. Needless to say, I'm *very* happy that I listened to my gut and got to know my dear friend, Harry.

People have asked me, "How do I know if I should just suck it up or go with what I'm feeling?" First, I will say that we have to examine our feelings. When I'm referring to a *gut feeling*, it's a deep intuition about something that quietly presses you *toward* something good or *away* from something dangerous. This is different than a feeling of, say, frustration, annoyance, or fatigue. Here's a chart to guide you with these decisions:

SHOULD I SUCK IT UP OR LISTEN TO MY GUT?

Different Scenarios	Suck It Up	Listen to Your Gut
You're working for extended hours but it's a job you really like	✓	
You're dealing with a demanding, high-standards client but the projects are interesting	✓	
You're expected to do things that are at odds with your moral compass		✓
Your boss is an egotist—but she is pro in her field and you're learning a lot	✓	
You dread Mondays for more than six months		✓

What's your gut telling you lately regarding your career? Is it prompting you in any particular way? Is it telling you to:

- Stop doing something?
- Get to the bottom of something?
- Have a certain conversation?
- Take charge of a situation?
- Learn more about something?
- Hire someone?
- Not hire someone?
- Take an interview?
- Work on something about yourself?
- Move on?
- Stay and become a source of positive leadership?

Please always consider what your gut, your second brain, is trying to tell you. It knows.

FINANCIAL FREEDOM

Financial freedom means that you get to make life decisions without being overly stressed about the financial impact—because you are prepared. You want to be in a position where you control your finances, instead of being controlled by them. This will put you in a place of empowerment—having the freedom to make a career change or to leave a lousy job vs. being handcuffed to a toxic work or life situation. This will serve to build your Moxie Muscle.

There are so many valuable resources to help guide you on this *freedom mission.* I have included what I consider to be the best of the best, and have added a few of my own personal nuggets. A big shout-out to millennialmoney.com and to daveramsey.com for their insights:

- Track where your money is going each month—this is a *very* revealing exercise.
- Pay yourself first—set aside a predetermined portion of your income the day you get paid, before you spend any discretionary money. (Unfortunately, what many people do is only save if something is left over. That's called paying yourself last.)
- Live on less than you make—avoid credit card debt at all costs.
- Have a six-month living expense *reserve* in the bank. This will give you the freedom to leave a bad work situation. Bestselling author Dan Lok writes about this in his book, *F.U. Money.*
- Think of yourself as an *investor*, not a consumer.
- Break the habit of instant gratification—it's much more rewarding to save up for something.
- Don't make a big purchase unless you sleep on it first—how do you feel about it in the morning, when the adrenaline surge has passed?
- Don't buy so much stuff—no one will want it anyway when you're ready to move or downsize.
- Do what you *love*—it won't feel like work, and the money will follow.
- Improve your *career value*—build a resume and skill set that's highly marketable.
- Build a side-hustle—what else can you do to *add* to your top line?
- Know your net worth—this is what you are worth when you add up your assets (what you own) and subtract your debt/liabilities.

REFRAMING VS. REHASHING

I find that women tend to be very hard on themselves. I'm certainly guilty of it. We can get stuck and obsess over negative things for hours and hours—what someone said, how someone treated us, mistakes we've made. This rehashing is a form of *self-induced torture.* The method that I use to get a grip on this negative rehashing is referred to as reframing.

Simply stated, reframing is taking the same facts but intentionally looking at them from a different perspective. When you're trying to halt a negative narrative from cycling through your head, this *different perspective* should be from a more positive and beneficial angle. This method is designed to direct your mind *out* of that bad place of thinking the worst *into* a good and peaceful place. There will be things in life that you can't control but you can control how you *react* to a situation. Reframing is a method that allows you to control of how you *react* to these situations.

What's happening during the reframing process is referred to as The Law of Substitution. This law affirms that our brains can only hold onto *one thought at a time.* When you make your brain consider the new, more positive narrative—it's forced to release the negative narrative that's been cycling through your mind.

Here are two examples of reframing at work:

Example #1

You were laid off. Your mind is rehashing thoughts like: *Why me? What am I going to do? This is awful!*

> Reframing narrative: "Getting laid off is terrifying but maybe it's the *jolt* I needed to move on. There's that position that I've been researching and daydreaming about over the past six months. I have enough money in the bank, plus the severance I received, to manage for at least four months. The job market's strong in this region. I'm going to be fine. It's scary, but I'm going to make this work."

Example #2

The boss that you really get along with has moved on to another position or company. You're devastated. Your mind is rehashing thoughts like: *What am I going to do?! There's never going to be anyone like her! She really cared about me and my career. I'm so screwed!*

> Reframing narrative: "Wow. This is going to be a big adjustment. I'm really going to miss her, but having a new manager will probably mean new thinking and new approaches that I can learn. New leaders can also have different connections within the company that could help me in the future. If I find that I'm not learning from my new boss, I will not be a victim. I can find a new job. I could even reach out to my prior boss to see if she has anything for me. I will definitely stay in touch with her."

When your new narrative is more positive and also *just* as plausible as the negative one, it will become your *replacement narrative*. With effective reframing, your rehashing attack can be resolved rather quickly, oftentimes in a flash—especially if you're motivated to seek an avenue for gaining this peace of mind.

There will be times when you'll have to keep working at it—repeating your replacement narrative in order to override the negative one. If you're determined to be strong *and* if you flex that Moxie Muscle of yours—you *will* be able to get unstuck. You may have to recruit the help of a family member or a friend. We'll discuss specifically how they can help you shortly.

There are some people, like my husband, who can "compartmentalize" negative thoughts and situations. I'm sure you know some of these people too. (They're usually guys.) They seem to be able to literally push disturbing thoughts and situations into a vault, or a little box of some kind, somewhere deep in their minds. Then, off they go, completely at peace, eating, sleeping, and heading back to work as if nothing happened.

But if you're like me, and *not* one of those people, I recommend that you practice and master reframing to have the peace of mind that you need and deserve. The practice of reframing can be one of the most powerful Moxie Muscle tools in your toolbox.

Below are some different techniques that have worked for me. Some of them are classic reframing, others are a bit more organic, but all of them can shift you back into high gear.

REFRAMING TECHNIQUES

Four questions to ask yourself to spark a more positive perspective

Ask yourself: How can I use this pain that I am experiencing as a future source of creativity and wisdom?
Remind yourself: Our greatest achievements and breakthroughs are often sparked from something painful that happened in our life.

Ask yourself: How can I take this source of *failure* as a learning that I can apply in the future?
Remind yourself: There will *always* be another chance to apply what you learned in the future—and you will feel really good when it happens.

Ask yourself: How did I *contribute* to this situation?
Remind yourself: When you take ownership of your role in a situation, you force your thought process to move *from* rehashing *to* problem-solving.

Ask yourself: Will this have *any* impact or value for me in the future?
Remind yourself: The answer to this question is usually no. So let it go. Shake it off. Imagine yourself putting it into the shredder or flushing it down the toilet or throwing it over a cliff.

Other ways to flip that rehashing switch to OFF

- **Depersonalize**: Tell yourself that the person who said something rude or negative is probably having a bad day—remind yourself that it's their problem, not yours. Don't take it in. Let it bounce off your new thick skin.
- **Have a Courageous Conversation**: Ask the person who has done something disturbing/annoying/hurtful if they have a minute to talk through this recent encounter. Oftentimes, you will find that they aren't even aware of the impact of their words or actions, and, frequently, what they said wasn't what they really meant. Clear the air as soon as you're able to speak calmly.
- **Distraction**: Go to the gym, take a vigorous walk, read a book, or do something that interests you. Remember that your mind can only hold onto one thought at a time,

so replace the rehashing with a *physical challenge* or with *new content* for your brain to focus on.

- **Enlist a trusted source to give you the opposing view**: Seek out someone you trust, but who won't coddle you. Brief them on the encounter that disturbed you, and have them take the side of your "opponent." (I recruit my husband, Marc, to do this with me all the time.) I can guarantee you that when you hear the other person's perspective *from someone you trust*, it will be much easier to accept. What will follow is a quieted mind.

I can't stress enough how much these reframing techniques have made a difference in my life. They are a source of peace of mind and they provide the distance and objectivity that I need to switch *off* rehashing attacks.

Over the years, before I learned how to leverage reframing, I lost a lot of precious time that I'll never get back. Don't let this happen to you. I love author LeAura Alderson's take on the value of reframing:

> "Reframe your frustrations into learnings and your earnings will grow."

MOXIE MUSCLE VOLTA MOMENTS

As you think about your Moxie Muscle, write on the lines below whether you have experienced any illuminations regarding:

- The benefits of your VOLTA To-Do List
- The thickness of your work skin
- If you are listening to your second brain
- If you are moving toward financial freedom
- If you are reframing vs. rehashing

____

____

____

ACTIONS

Declare below what you will start doing right away to strengthen your Moxie Muscle:

____

____

____

READY TO TURN TO PART 3

Now you have all the ingredients you will need to pull everything together—into your VOLTA career plan. This is the time in your VOLTA journey when you get to leverage the personal epiphanies that you gained in Part 1 with the awareness that you gleaned from your self-assessment surveys from Part 2. I'll help you put it all together in a roadmap that lays out a step-by-step plan for putting your career into high gear.

The only person who can stop you now is you!

PART 3

READY, SET, VOLTA

CREATING YOUR OWN VOLTA CAREER PLAN

“Your desire
to change
must be
greater than
your desire
to stay
the same.”

ANONYMOUS

MANY OF YOU ARE READING *Career VOLTA* because you're ready for something more. Perhaps you want to get unstuck, to be more promotable, or you might want to make a career change.

No matter what your reason is, you're now ready to roll up your sleeves and create your VOLTA Career Plan.

Note: To help you along, there is a completed sample VOLTA Career Plan that you can follow in the Appendix.

You must come mentally prepared to push out of the autopilot state that you're probably functioning in. (Our brains love autopilot—that's where they want us to stay—because our brains don't like change.) Life coaches often refer to the process of moving out of this mode as "trance-formational." It's when you break free from the "trance" that you're in—when you become conscious of your unconscious—that you can start the process of designing your future.

You are about to create a different narrative for your career life—one that will open you up to new possibilities.

Take in these words of wisdom from NYC financier Ziad Abdelnour:

> "Just because the past didn't turn out like you wanted it to, doesn't mean that your future can't be better than you ever imagined."

Your VOLTA Career Plan components

You are going to incorporate everything you learned from Parts 1 and 2 into your personalized action plan. Your plan will be highly doable and satisfying. It will be shaped to align with *your* vision and goals—that *you* set for yourself. Your VOLTA Career Plan will serve as the roadmap for taking you from where you are today to where you want to be in 6–12 months.

First, I will help you crystallize the clearest possible picture of your desired **future self** by helping you to formulate a clear vision of what your transformed career life will look like and feel like.

You will then take inventory of where you are today—your **current self.** Remember the epiphanies that you've had along the way, and the honest self-assessments you made? We will capture all of these in one place, and they will give you the clear picture that you need for setting the basis of your current reality.

To make this transformation from your current self to your desired future self, I will help you identify and *close the gaps*, paving the way to the fulfillment of your wants and wishes—to greater promotability and career advancement—with the confidence to make it happen.

ENVISIONING YOUR FUTURE SELF

As you prepare for the transformation from your current self to your future self, it is vital that you formulate a clear picture of your future self. Envisioning your future self is one of those rare times in your life that you purposely think about what you really want.

This is the time when you get to ask yourself what bestselling author Laurie Beth Jones poses in her book, *The Path*:

> “If all things were possible, what would you be doing with your life?”

To find your answer, I'm going to have you mentally project into the future to visualize yourself...where you are happier and more fulfilled in your career life. We will do this by leveraging three different methods to help you gain better clarity about your future career self. Feel free to pick any of the options that appeals to you the most—or try them all out!

FUTURE SELF VISUALIZATION

Simply close your eyes and imagine yourself—visualize yourself—in your career, 6–12 months from now. Think about these questions and jot down everything that's *appealing to you* in your future self reflection:

- What burdens have been lifted from your days?
- What are your primary roles and responsibilities?
- What are you no *longer* doing?
- What are you still doing?
- What *new and different* things are you now doing?
- What does your workspace look like?
- Where are you working now? Same company? Different company?
- Are you living/working in the same geography, or have you moved?
- Are you working alone or on a team?
- Who's on your team? What is your role on the team?
- What's your team's mission?

____

____

____

____

____

____

CREATING A VISION BOARD

For this next method, you will select *images* from magazines, catalogues, and Pinterest that represent an element or feeling that you want to experience in your career 6–12 months from now.

Select words or images that capture:

- What you are doing or accomplishing
- Who you are interacting with
- Where you are working
- How you are feeling
- What you are wearing
- What you are building or creating
- What problems you are solving
- What your workspace looks like
- What your free time looks like
- What your family life looks like

Tape or pin these words and images onto a surface that you can see, on a frequent basis, to keep your eye on the prize.

ENVISIONING YOUR IDEAL JOB

For some people, creating a job description of their "ideal job" is the most motivating way to crystallize a portrayal of their future self. Create your ideal job description by listing:

- Your company's mission
- Your primary roles and responsibilities
- Required skills
- What's not required
- Leveraged gifts/strengths
- Your typical day/week
- Who you work with

- Your clients
- % travel

Projecting yourself into your future state—no matter which method(s) you use—is a powerful way to get your brain to start the process of re-imagining a new future for yourself. You should start to feel some excitement building on the inside. Exactly what is it that excites you about this? Is there anything holding you back? Most importantly, what is your heart saying? Our heart holds the key to change. So think of yourself as an empowered change-agent—on a mission, in the driver's seat—and follow your heart as you purposely head toward the new vision that you have for your career. This is *not* the time to listen to your brain.

TURNING YOUR VISION INTO A GOAL STATEMENT

Now that you have crystallized the picture and defined features of what your ideal career looks like and feels like, it's time to roll it up into a concrete, measurable goal statement.

A goal statement that embodies your vision should have three components:

- Alignment with a need
- Timing
- Specificity

Needs include categories such as security, stability, control, freedom, visibility, leadership, recognition, influence, creativity, achievement, relationships, to be of service, to be listened to, to be needed, to be included, to experience a connection to something greater than oneself.

Here are some examples of goal statements that incorporate the three components of a need, timing, and specificity:

- I need to be in a leadership position to influence business decisions—so over the next 6–12 months I will enhance my stock and tenaciously pursue my promotion to Marketing Director.
- I need more visibility—so over the next 6 months I will seek out a higher-level position at the company headquarters.
- I need to listen to my gut instinct, to have more time with my loved ones—so in 12 months I will no longer work as a management consultant. I will seek a position with a local organization that leverages my talents and cuts down on my travel time.
- I need to feel in control of my creative choices—so with the help of my VOLTA To-Do list, in 6 months I will have secured five freelance projects, and will be primed to strike out on my own, with a thriving roster of clients, by the end of the year.

Write down your goal statement in the box provided. Be sure to start with the need you are determined to fulfill, with timing, and the specifics of your goal.

Make sure your goal:

- Is reasonably possible
- Depends mostly on your choices vs. anyone else's choices
- Is something you care enough about to make it a priority (in other words, it's at least a 7 on a scale of 1 to 10)
- Has a specific timeline

My 6–12 month career goal

The specific need that I'm going to fulfill is...

So, in 6–12 months, I will...

Ask yourself where your goal statement ranks on a scale of 1 to 10. It should be something that gets you very excited, so if it's not a 7 or higher on the scale below, you owe it to yourself to reexamine the essence of your goal statement.

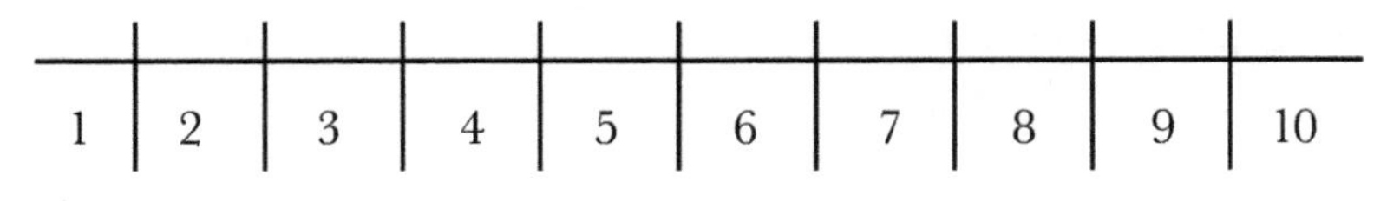

Ho-hum

It's a "Wow!"

TAKING STOCK OF YOUR CURRENT SELF

The time has come for you to take stock of your baseline—your current self—as an assessment of where things stand *today* in your career life. Think of this part of the process as capturing the facts, just the facts. In the next section, you will work on mapping out solutions.

In the box that follows, document the facts of your current situation. No overthinking. No self-judgment. Just write down free-flowing notes on your current situation.

Current self

Overall, related to my work life, this is my current state of mind...

YOUR CURRENT SELF GAP ASSESSMENT

Now you are going to jot down some quick answers to several gap-seeking questions. These gaps will relate to your overall situation, your limiting beliefs, your energy-drainers, your skills, and how you are projecting and connecting. It's important to surface these gaps so they can be dealt with in order to achieve your vision and goals.

Overall situation

- What events or choices in my life have led me to this place in my career?

  ____

  ____

- If I could wave a magic wand and change one thing about my career life, what would that be? Why?

  ____

  ____

- What are the three things that I want to change in the next 90 days?

  ____

  ____

- What are the three things that I like/love about my current career?

  ____

  ____

- And here's a question for the brave of heart: What is the person that I envy doing in their career life? (Answering this question can be very uncomfortable, but rather revealing.)

  ____

  ____

Limiting beliefs

- What beliefs do I have about myself that might be getting in the way of my career vision?

  ____

  ____

- What work-related fears and stressors am I currently struggling with?

  ____

  ____

- How is my internal dialogue impacting me on the job these days?

  ____

  ____

- Is my *mindset* status at work, Camp I'm Hard On Myself or Camp I'm Still Learning? Is it set to help me or to hinder me? Explain.

___

___

Energy-drainers

- What are the three things that are draining my energy in my current position?

___

___

- What are the three things that are giving me energy in my current position?

___

___

- What changes would make my work more of an adventure vs. a drudgery?

___

___

- Do I have the *Moxie Muscle* I need to keep my work-based struggles at a healthy distance?

___

___

Skills

- What skills do I need to improve or acquire to actualize my vision?

____

____

- How's my current level of on-the-job *GRAVITAS*?

____

____

- Where am I with respect to earning my seat at *The Table*?

____

____

- How comfortable am I with having work-related *Courageous Conversations*?

____

____

- Am I on the *me*-side of the leadership line or have I crossed over to the *them*-side?

____

____

- How am I leveraging the benefits of *reframing*? Explain.

____

____

Projecting and connecting

- How would my coworkers describe me as a *brand*?

____

____

- What have I learned that I'm projecting—that might be off-putting at work?

____

____

- What needs to change about me for my career dreams to be achieved?

____

____

READY TO CREATE YOUR VOLTA CAREER PLAN

Now it's time to put all of this together into *your* VOLTA Career Plan. You've identified and declared your *why*, crystallized a vision of your future self, written your goal statement, captured your current baseline, and identified your gaps. You've done a lot!

It's time to combine all of these ingredients and get your life-enriching VOLTA Career Plan down on paper. What follows is a handy template that you will fill out—this will serve as your roadmap, your own personalized plan to a career reimagined.

Essentially, this template will help you to tie together all of the epiphanies that you've had on this journey into your reimagined career work plan. You will have an all-in-one plan that includes your vision and career goal—with the gaps that you need to address—complete with specific action steps and timelines.

Remember the famous saying that Rome wasn't built in a day? Apply this thinking to your plan. You'll have a much higher probability of success if you take small, steady steps toward your goal vs. trying to do it in one giant leap. It will feel a lot more manageable, and it will be a lot more productive.

Creating your VOLTA Career Plan should take *less than an hour.* You'll want to choose the best time and place to do this, so you can give it your full attention and your best thinking. **I have also included a filled-out sample plan, in the Appendix, so that you have something to reference as you create your personalized plan.**

It's go-time!

MY VOLTA CAREER PLAN

My future self vision

Write down some notes or a bulleted list—whatever form captures the essence—of the most important and most appealing descriptions of what your future self is doing in "her" career. You should feel *limitless* as you're doing this.

(Refer to your visualization/vision board/ideal job description notes on pages 152-154.)

My career goal

Write down your goal statement—be sure that it starts off with what you truly need in your career life going forward, that it's specific, and that it scores a 7 or higher on a scale of 1–10. Your goal statement should stir you up—it should make you feel excited and ready to get moving.

(Refer to your 6–12 month career goal on page 156.)

My *why*

Write down your *why*—the unstoppable force that is driving you toward your transformed career life.

(Refer to My *why* on page 4.)

My success gaps

We all have gaps–obstacles and hurdles that we need to address in order to reach our career dreams. These gaps generally fall into five categories: Limiting Beliefs, Behaviors, Energy-Drainers, Skills, and Moxie Muscle. You will need to consider and examine all of these five categories as you craft your VOLTA Career Plan.

(Refer to your Gap Assessment on pages 158-162.)

LIMITING BELIEFS

This category includes things like your mindset, your inner dialogue, and your fears and stressors.

Focus on your **top 3 limiting beliefs**—that will make the biggest impact on you reaching your career goal.

LIMITING BELIEF #1

Action step:

Start date:

LIMITING BELIEF #2

Action step:

Start date:

LIMITING BELIEF #3

Action step:

Start date:

BEHAVIORS

This category captures what you will want to address as you consider yourself as *a brand* in your work life. What are the things that you're projecting and how you are connecting with others that require attention and correction in order to reach your career goal?

Focus on your **top 3 behaviors**—that will make the biggest impact on you reaching your career goal.

BEHAVIOR #1

Action step:

Start date:

BEHAVIOR #2

Action step:

Start date:

BEHAVIOR #3

Action step:

Start date:

ENERGY-DRAINERS

This category includes all of the things that bring you down—people, places, and situations that *drain* you. They may cause you to walk on eggshells, or may give you a sense that you don't belong. They can also set off an alarm bell in your gut.

Focus on your **top 3 energy-drainers**—that, when resolved, will make the biggest impact on you reaching your career goal.

ENERGY-DRAINER #1

Action step:

Start date:

ENERGY-DRAINER #2

Action step:

Start date:

ENERGY-DRAINER #3

Action step:

Start date:

SKILLS

There are two types of skills that can impact your performance—interpersonal skills AND technical skills—and both matter. Be sure to consider things like your current level of skill with GRAVITAS, having a seat at The Table, Leadership, Courageous Conversations, and doing the homework to stand out. Don't forget about the technical skills—those industry-specific skills that you need to get that promotion.

Focus on your **top 3 skills**—that will make the biggest impact on you reaching your career goal.

SKILL #1

Action step:

Start date:

SKILL #2

Action step:

Start date:

SKILL #3

Action step:

Start date:

MOXIE MUSCLE

This category relates to your ability to view work-related matters from a healthy distance. When you can be more objective, you will gain a better ability to shake things off. Consider your VOLTA To-Do list, wearing your thick skin to work, trusting your gut, making financial freedom your mission, and leveraging reframing.

Focus on your **top 3 Moxie Muscle** weaknesses— that will make the biggest impact on you reaching your career goal.

MOXIE MUSCLE #1

Action step:

Start date:

MOXIE MUSCLE #2

Action step:

Start date:

MOXIE MUSCLE #3

Action step:

Start date:

NOW YOU'RE UNSTOPPABLE

Congratulations! You have accomplished what few people have ever achieved. You've made it your business to do the reflection, the self-assessment, and the work to become the CEO of your life.

You should now be in what I call *resolve mode.* When someone is resolved, she is taking action that is characterized as being "firmly set on a purpose" and "determined." When someone is resolved, she is *unstoppable.*

Are *you* ready to be unstoppable?

When I'm in resolve mode, I know that the people around me can feel it. They know that something has happened. That something about me has changed.

Own this frame of mind for yourself by committing to live by these words from bestselling author Ayn Rand:

> “The question isn’t who is going to *let me*, it’s who is going to *stop me.*”

There’s one other key ingredient to be unstoppable and ensure that your dream will be realized—and that is *staying power.* Staying power is achieved through accountability and commitment to your VOLTA Career Plan.

Here are some quick pointers to help you have the staying power you will need to stick with your VOLTA Career Plan:

- **Tackle the easiest steps first.** This will give you forward momentum right out of the gate. When you quickly take action on these easier steps, you will have what’s referred to as “early wins.” Apply this strategy to how you tackle your plan.
- **Review each of your steps to ensure clarity.** Be sure that you know exactly what you have to do to complete each one. Steps that are obscure or too vague will throw you off track and lead to confidence-robbing delays.
- **Ask yourself if each step is something you can commit to.** Be sure for each step that you can say, *I know that I will do this.* If you find that you’ve included a step you’re not certain that you can commit to, break it down into smaller, less intimidating pieces OR understand the why behind your inability to commit to that step, and then replace it with something that you can commit to.

- **Make sure your timeline for each step is realistic.** It's better to take a bit more time vs. facing a sense of failure or defeat for not hitting your dates.
- **Give yourself a reward.** As you complete each of your action steps, give yourself a reward—maybe a massage, or buy yourself a new accessory–anything that helps you celebrate your achievements.

As you start to live out your VOLTA Career Plan, I strongly recommend that you enlist the help of a trusted person to be your *accountability advocate*—someone to check in with over coffee each month, to review your progress with. This person has to be someone that you trust and respect—someone who is a cheerleader, with a track record of being very honest with you.

Seek out a mentor, someone who you can learn from. Ideally, your mentor is in a position to watch you *in action* so they are better able to give you constructive feedback on things that you need to improve.

Some people choose to hire a career coach. I did, and I found it empowering to be supported by someone who had my back *and* who helped me to stay on track. Life coaching is a fast-emerging field. There are many qualified life coaches who specialize in career development that are available to help you with this process. You can find them on Google and LinkedIn. It's a great birthday present to yourself.

Your investment in yourself shouldn't happen just once–even once a year isn't enough. Invest in yourself on a consistent basis to sharpen your thinking and to broaden your skills. This can be done by taking courses, attending seminars, reading books. Stay ahead of the pack by immersing yourself in various hot topics such as: innovations in your industry and related industries, self-improvement, and leadership.

Investing in yourself and continuing to prioritize your plan is your best insurance policy against letting "benign neglect" take root. You've worked too hard to let things just slip away. Have frequent progress check-ins with yourself and your accountability advocate to stay committed to realizing your career dreams. Please don't become one of those people who have to face the heartache of regret down the road.

PARTING THOUGHTS

I take a great deal of inspiration from Diana Nyad. She became the first person to swim from Cuba to Florida–103 miles in shark-infested waters–without a protective cage. What really blows me away is that she tried it four times over a 35-year period and failed due to complicating factors such as jellyfish stings, strong currents and winds, and asthma. But she didn't give up. She found a way. It was on her fifth attempt, at the age of 64, when she finally made it to a Key West beach–*willing her way* for 53 hours straight. This is her heartfelt guidance to us as we press on, facing and overcoming the challenges and the obstacles in our own lives as we follow our dreams:

> "None of us ever get through this life without heartache, without turmoil, but if you believe and have faith, you can find your way."

This passage is a perfect way to close out our VOLTA journey together. Please visit me at **www.VOLTAlife.org.**

Let's stay in touch!

SPECIAL THANKS

For several reasons, this should have been the worst year of my life. But it became one of the best years I could have ever imagined. I saw the greatness of God from the overwhelming outpouring of support and encouragement that I received from *all of you*. I am reminded of Psalm 23:5 from the Hebrew bible: "My cup runneth over."

I do not think of this book as my book. Because of all of the vibrant collaboration that came with writing and editing this book, I hold *Career VOLTA* in my heart as *our* book. Over 100 of us worked together–united in our fervor to help women find and cultivate the confidence and the skills they need to rise to their full potential in their careers. We know that it's not "something that you're born with" rather it's having that combination of courage, curiosity, and humility–to learn, to fail and to get back up and learn again.

First and foremost, I want to acknowledge **Erin McKnight**, my writing partner of 18 months. You are the most gracious and generous source of patience and forward momentum. We spent countless hours together "putting some dirt on the page" keeping things moving forward to get to the finish line. We were determined to pass this knowledge forward to other career women. Talk at 6:00am? No problem!

To my husband, my love, my **Marc.** You are my number one source of wisdom and adventure. You complete me.

Meredith, you are a treasure. How can someone so young be such a source of insight, savoir-faire and diplomacy? You're living proof that millennials should be asked questions and should be listened to.

Tom, thank you for giving me the confidence to tell my story. You always make me stronger. You gave me VOLTA.

Lynn and Forrest, I love you dearly. Thank you for your brilliance and for all of those Hollywood moments.

Rebecca, Danielle, Erez, and Patrick, your honesty and courage are priceless. You told me what was missing, what was weak, and how to fix it.

Roxana, you are a woman of vision, an unstoppable force. I'm very blessed to know you. You're an inspiration to so many.

Stef, you make *everything* better. I couldn't have done this without you. No way.

Yvonne and Tony, you believed in me from day one. This has kept me going. You made everything easier and you helped me laugh at myself. Much love to you both.

JuLee Brand (book cover designer), you are masterful. How many authors can say the "winning book cover" was in the first round? You work with such ease, grace and respect. You are a force, a shining light for many.

Niño Gallego (photographer), your determination to capture *that something special* is striking. Your humble, deeply creative soul is palpable and something to behold.

Ellen Peixoto and **Anita Taylor** (editors), your perseverance and unstoppable quest for excellence is impressive!

I'm deeply grateful to the *Career VOLTA* Launch Team for their time, feedback, and insight that brought value and inspiration to the book. I hope *Career VOLTA* serves as a confidence-building touchstone for all women on their journey to career advancement and joy.

Kathy Anderson
Stef Angeli
Alexandra Appolonia
Jennifer Asselin
Roxana Bannach-Lin
Joy Bastelli
Lauren Bastelli
Ellie Bettenstedt
Jennifer Bittner
Tania Bomtempo
Taylor Bradley
Chris Brand
JuLee Brand
Ariella Joy Brant
Laura Burrough
Kim Burtner
Tara Carothers
Colleen Carter
Robin Clark
Janis Cracolici
Jill Cruz
Nicole Dolan
Kyleigh Dooley
Macey Dooley
Christine Dziubinsky
Alyssa Eckert
Mackenzie English
Renate English
Leslee Epperhart
Lori Eslick
Adrienne Felder
Elex Fitzgerald
Jillian Gaumond
Heidi Gearhart
Daria Georgiyeva
Vic Goodman
Emily Grove
Isabella Grove
Patrick Harney
Robin Harney
Debra Hartwick
Kristin Herbert
Melissa Hernandez
Katherine Hurley
Liz Hurley
Sarah Hyde
Melissa Joyce
Erez Kalir
Cindi Kane
John Keenan
Leah Keenan
Robin Keener
Theresa Keil
Nina Kosoglou
Jessica Kraus
Dalaiah Kusner
Blanca Lindabery
Christina Lombardo
Cyndi Loo
Danielle Lurie
Cara Macksoud
Coral Mags
Jenn Main
Michele McKee
Andrew McKnight
Erin McKnight
Dana Mitra
Christine Montagna
Natalie Moore
Pamela Moore
Mary Moran
Meredith Moran
Sarah Moran
Allie Moss
Tony Moss
Yvonne Moss
Lindsay Nahum
Trudy Olsen
Ellen Peixoto
Tom Phillips
Stephanie Puglisi
Cory Regovich
Susan Robertson
Gillian Scarpino
Barbara Schliep
Rebekka Schliep
Jean Scully
Amare Silva
Jeniffer Singley
Vivian Taormina

Anita Taylor
Laura Taylor
Terri Tirrell
Morgan Thomas
Jill Tropea
Courtney Valerio
Josephine VanHouten
Abi Vetter
Betsy Wadsworth
Hilary Waks
Dianne Waters
Marilyn Whetstone
Abbi Williams
Buzz Woods
Tammy Wright
Amanda Yarnell
KC Yoon
Jackie Yursha
Kristin Yursha
Lisa Zimmerman
Allison Zucosky

APPENDIX

PROJECTING CONFIDENCE ASSESSMENT

DOES SHE:	NEVER	ALMOST NEVER	SOMETIMES	ALMOST ALWAYS	ALWAYS
Enter a room with purpose?	1	2	3	4	5
Convey warmth?	1	2	3	4	5
Look into people's eyes?	1	2	3	4	5
Stand tall?	1	2	3	4	5
Deliberately occupy your space?	1	2	3	4	5
Have a firm handshake?	1	2	3	4	5
Bring forward an informed POV?	1	2	3	4	5
Ask informed questions?	1	2	3	4	5
Feel comfortable saying no?	1	2	3	4	5
Embrace self-compassion?	1	2	3	4	5
Have a curiosity-based mindset?	1	2	3	4	5

PROJECTING LEADERSHIP ASSESSMENT

DOES SHE:	NEVER	ALMOST NEVER	SOMETIMES	ALMOST ALWAYS	ALWAYS
Paint a picture of the end goal?	1	2	3	4	5
Say "we" more than "I"?	1	2	3	4	5
Take responsibility for things?	1	2	3	4	5
Give credit to others?	1	2	3	4	5
Bring can-do solutions?	1	2	3	4	5
Bring calm to tense situations?	1	2	3	4	5
Have tough conversations?	1	2	3	4	5
Coach people on what needs to improve?	1	2	3	4	5
View setbacks as learnings?	1	2	3	4	5

PROJECTING OFF-PUTTING BEHAVIORS ASSESSMENT

DOES SHE:	NEVER	ALMOST NEVER	SOMETIMES	ALMOST ALWAYS	ALWAYS
Say "I" more than "we"?	1	2	3	4	5
Interrupt as people are explaining?	1	2	3	4	5
Use the word "but" when responding?	1	2	3	4	5
Debate to gain agreement?	1	2	3	4	5
Secretly need to be the smartest person in the room?	1	2	3	4	5
Convey closed-off body language?	1	2	3	4	5
Come off aggressively via her voice or body language?	1	2	3	4	5
Tend to assign blame?	1	2	3	4	5
Defend her position?	1	2	3	4	5
Feel like it's just better to do it herself?	1	2	3	4	5

CONNECTING WITH OTHERS ASSESSMENT

DOES SHE:	NEVER	ALMOST NEVER	SOMETIMES	ALMOST ALWAYS	ALWAYS
Actively listen to what is being said?	1	2	3	4	5
Listen to what is *not* being said?	1	2	3	4	5
Take note of others' body language?	1	2	3	4	5
Seek out common ground?	1	2	3	4	5
Put herself in other people's shoes?	1	2	3	4	5
Leverage questions as a way to connect on a deeper level?	1	2	3	4	5
Let people save face when they make a mistake?	1	2	3	4	5
Leverage humor to lighten the mood?	1	2	3	4	5
Convey a relaxing aura through her body language?	1	2	3	4	5
Believe that people are trying to do their best?	1	2	3	4	5

SAMPLE VOLTA CAREER PLAN

MY FUTURE SELF VISION

- *I have been promoted to Marketing Director of the Respiratory/Allergy Team. Reporting to me are four Product Managers.*
- *We are a well-oiled, highly collaborative team—known for hitting and exceeding our quarterly sales/market share goals—because we are totally immersed in the nuances of our marketplace.*
- *People want to be on my team—I am known as a good mentor. I'm able to have honest conversations with them that help improve their performance and their promotability.*
- *I am more aware of the impact of my words on my team.*
- *I have become a persuasive presenter—because of this, I have a great track record of getting senior leadership to grant us the budget we need to invest further into our brands.*
- *At the National Thought-Leadership Conference, I am now "putting myself out there," so I'm able to build mutually productive relationships with key industry decision-makers.*
- *I am actively reprogramming my inner dialogue, and I'm busting out of my perfectionist mindset.*
- *I am spending less time with the negative people at my workplace.*
- *I am sleeping better at night—because I am getting a lot better at creating some "distance" between my business-related challenges and my personal life.*
- *I'm paying better attention to my gut instincts.*
- *I've made it a daily "habit" to spend 10 minutes updating my hardworking to-do list!*

MY CAREER GOAL

I need more visibility and the ability to influence business decisions—so over the next 6–12 months I will enhance my stock and tenaciously pursue my promotion to Marketing Director.

MY *WHY*

I want to prove to myself that I'm capable of achieving anything that I set my mind to, even if it feels impossible!

MY SUCCESS GAPS

LIMITING BELIEFS #1

I don't think my inner dialogue is helping me to pursue my (kinda scary) quest for this promotion.

- Action step: *I will mindfully do a one-week audit of my inner dialogue to assess what it is saying. I will write down my findings and I will work on replacement statements to counter any negative, repeating thoughts.*

- Start date: *Next week—starting on Monday, March 19th*

LIMITING BELIEFS #2

Having to be "perfect," which is causing me to have a defensive mindset—I feel like I have to be right all the time.

- Action step: *Every time I feel/hear myself slip into Camp A, I'm hard on myself mode, I will remind myself that I'm an*

evolving "learner"—and in this setting, I will silently repeat to myself, "Bring it on. This is fun!"
- *I will read* Mindset *by Carol S. Dweck and* The Gifts of Imperfection *by Brené Brown*

- Start date: *Every time I need it.*

BEHAVIOR #1

I have to start being more aware that "I am a brand," but I'm not exactly sure what I might be doing that's off-putting to my colleagues.

- Action step: *I will ask 10 people I work with to fill out the* Career VOLTA *Assessment.*

- Start date: *Over the next 2–3 weeks, I will make a list of 10 names of people I know who will be honest with me and I will approach each of them, individually over coffee or lunch, and share this exercise with them to get their feedback. I will complete these surveys by the end of April. I will create an action plan to address any "discoveries" that these survey findings reveal.*

BEHAVIOR #2

I tend to interrupt people, and I'm probably not listening closely enough to what people are saying and what they are not saying (their body language).

- Action step: *I will stop myself from interrupting, and I will turn my phone over in meetings in order to focus on what is being said—and to observe clues and signals from others' body language.*
  - *I will read* Just Listen *by Mark Goulston*

- Start date: *Starting today!*

BEHAVIOR #3

I'm realizing that I function more in the "me-side" vs. the "them-side" at work.

- Action step: *Listen carefully to how I phrase things to be on the alert for me-focused language. Also I will be more in touch with my motivations—are they team-driven or me-driven?*
- Start date: *Starting now.*

ENERGY-DRAINER #1

There are people at work who I'm spending time with that are dragging me down. They see this as a job vs. a career—and they are constantly negative.

- Action step: *Stop having lunch with Max and Christine—take a mental health walk at lunchtime instead.*
- Start date: *I will start my walks next week. This week I will give Max and Christine a heads-up about starting my daily walks at lunch so that I can "clear my head."*

ENERGY-DRAINER #2

I have become very lax with my morning workouts and my no-sugar food plan, so lately I'm waking up in a bad state of mind. I'm feeling really bummed out.

- Action step: *Press the re-start button—text Steve and re-up my training sessions. Clear out the fridge and pantry—I know exactly what has to go!*
  - *I will read* The Blood Sugar Solution *by Mark Hyman, MD*
- Start date: *After vacation!*

ENERGY-DRAINER #3

My commute to work is killing me! The traffic is getting worse every day. I've grown weary of life in the suburbs.

- Action step: *Figure out my options for relocating to a place with a vibrant town center (within walking distance) that's near public transportation—and near the company.*
- Start date: *Research options in March/April, find a realtor by May, list my house by June, relocate to a town that meets my requirements for a "new season in life" by no later than next spring.*

SKILL #1

I want to have more gravitas. I need to purposely occupy more space. I want to have more presence in business social settings—connect faster.

- Action step: *I will perfect my firm handshake and warm eye contact at client meetings. I will think about 2–3 questions that I can ask of new business contacts to get to know them on a deeper level.*
  - *I will read* Executive Presence *by Sylvia Ann Hewlett*
- Start date: *Will give it a try at next week's client meeting, and at the upcoming Thought-Leader Conference this spring*

SKILL #2

I will make it my business to become a persuasive presenter.

- Action step: *I will do some research to find a presentation coach or course that my company is willing to sponsor. If I have to, I will invest in myself—it's critical that I become a persuasive speaker to be a Marketing Director.*

- *I will read* Out Front *by Deborah Shames*

- Start date: *I will sign up for a presentation skills seminar or hire a coach by the end of May.*

SKILL #3

I am determined to stand out and earn my seat at The Table with clients and upper management.

- Action step: *I will do my 15–30 minutes daily power sessions, catch up on all of my clients' recent market research decks—and subscribe to the top three publications most relevant to my marketplace. I will add value and compelling ideas during upcoming meetings.*

- Start date: *Subscriptions to pubs will be placed by the end of this month. Start daily immersions then.*

SKILL #4

I will start having important, courageous conversations.

- Action step: *I will consider all the conversations that I haven't had the courage to have (and have been avoiding). I will determine which ones are important to tackle asap.*
  - *I will read* Difficult Conversations *by Stone, Patton, and Heen*

- Start date: *Within four weeks, I will have identified and had the conversations that I've been avoiding. Going forward, I will have these conversations, as needed, on a very timely basis.*

MOXIE MUSCLE #1

I will be more in tune with my gut instincts.

- Action step: *Listen to my second brain whenever it's trying to tell me something.*

- Start date: *Starting today.*

MOXIE MUSCLE #2

I will make a habit out of doing a kickass to-do list, every day—that will help me keep the path to my promotion as a top priority.

- Action step: *Buy a new Moleskine to house this new hard-working to-do list!*

- Start date: *This weekend.*

MOXIE MUSCLE #3

I will deliberately be "fully on" or "fully off" when it comes to my work time and my family time—I will not try to juggle both at the same time!

- Action step: *Stop checking my work messages when I'm with my family—whether it's out to dinner during the week or when we are doing an activity together unless something urgent is brewing.*

- Start date: *Right now.*

MOXIE MUSCLE #4

I'm going to start limiting my beat-myself-up-sessions and I'm going to practice reframing—in the service of reducing my mentally draining rehashing.

- Action step: *I will actively monitor myself for episodes of rehashing. If necessary, I will start to wear a rubber band around my wrist to use as a reminder. I will also enlist the help of a trusted (and honest) friend or family member—to help me reframe my circular thinking with a plausible, but healthier perspective.*

- Start date: *Find the rubber band over the weekend.*
  - Reach out to my reframing partner within one month.